Self
Publishing
Made
Easy

D0126916

William Carroll

Coda Publications, San Marcos, CA 92079

Self Publishing Made Easy
By
William Carroll

First Edition
Copyright 1999 by William Carroll

Printed in the United States of America
ISBN 0-910390-63-0
Library of Congress Catalog Number 98-94786

Coda Publications
P.O.Bin 711
San Marcos, California 92079-0711, U.S.A.

Contents

About This Book

This is probably the most unusual writer's book you'll ever read because it does not presume to tell you how to write.

Be it an autobiography, a how-to, self-help, get better or massive reference work, this is a manual of self-publishing. As such it will do much to insure successful completion of your book's creation, design, pre-press production, printing, publication, publicity, marketing and profitability.

Writing you may already know better than others or can learn before or during your book's creation. Here we're going to explain how to actually publish and profit from the worth of your non-fiction writings. Early in this book I'll recommend a number

About This Book

of rather dull preliminary planning steps. By taking them in your stride there will be a generous measure of freedom from worry. Knowing that the many harassing details of publication are out of the way will encourage your creative juices to flow freely and productively.

Please keep in mind, that this is a guidebook along the pathway of successful self-publishing...not about writing or selling a book to another publisher, doing poetry or authoring novels. From the excitement of your original idea, through setting up a Table of Contents, writing a book to fit its niche in the market, negotiating an affordable printing contract, obtaining publicity and marketing your book; what you need to know is here. So read on, enjoy, and become a successful self-publisher of the book you plan to write or complete.

In this book you will find repetition now and then. This is needful because book publishing is a most complicated business and in a few instances I'll want you to worry about something in one chapter, plan to do something about it in the next chapter and finally do that something as your book nears completion. At least, I'll keep you from hunting back and forth for information needed when you're ready for action. At first such redundancy may be worth questioning but as you proceed the bits and pieces fall into place.

It's quite likely that at one time or another you've been exposed to lectures or books on writing and publishing. A question you may well ask of every person presenting their approach to book publishing is

About This Book

"So, where are you coming from and where are you going in the publishing business?"

Here are the answers, as they apply to me. In 1951 I entered the publishing field as managing editor of the book division of a major west coast publishing house. My staff and I produced in house, or purchased from outside authors, from four to eight titles a year. Print runs ranged from 125,000 to 175,000 copies of each title. The books were distributed to news-stands all over the United States and generally remained on sale for about 90 days. Those books that did not sell were returned to our warehouses and retailed by mail from advertising placed in the company's many monthly magazines.

After a few years of this education and experience, with no significant pay increases, I left to launch my own publishing companies. In sum total (as of 1999) my fingerprints are on about one hundred books. Some of these I've written, others were edited or produced for other publishers and many were purchased from independent authors for publishing through one or the other of my two successful publishing companies which were founded in 1955.

Concurrently, from 1955 through 1968, I traveled internationally as a journalist and book publisher in search of new material for the printed media. Plus being involved with creating and managing marketing programs for a number of national and global organizations. The variety was great and the money very interesting.

About This Book

From 1970 to 1983 I published three newspapers and managed to put out a few books during the same period. In current years the book publishing field has spread into supportive activities including the publication of maps, production of television programs, videos, computer games and books on computer disks. A reasonable proportion of these sidelines have been satisfactorily profitable...a few have been outstanding failures. No apologies.

That's business.

It's this background of experience that makes it possible for me to lecture and/or be a member of panel presentations covering the diverse aspects of the publishing business. This result, *Self Publishing Made Easy*, may be the only book you'll ever need to be a successful self-publisher.

For what it's worth, the book publishing business has been very good to me and I live a pleasant life. Lessons learned from it have proven most valuable. It may well be said that I'm willing to accept everything I hear and learn about publishing, while continuing to act selectively based on my best judgment and fond hopes.

At this point it's worth noting that about 80 percent of all published books barely break even: Read this as "Usually lose money." About 15 percent of published books show a reasonable profit and great sums of money are often made on the remaining five percent. Thankfully, in the latter group are many self-published books.

About This Book

So what is self-publishing. In general terms a self-published book stems from the creativity of a person with unusual interesting skills or knowledge. They reduce this valuable attribute to a book format, pay good money to have the book printed and trust to luck the public will respond and buy in quantity. Rarely do self-publishers do more than one book though a modest number of them have established an entire line of books based on the author/publisher's skills or knowledge. This latter group includes those happy individuals who find self-publishing a most attractive money-making enterprise. In addition more than one has expanded and moved into the trade publishing field by producing a number of titles on a variety of themes. In sum, any successful book (self-published or from a prestigious trade house) must have editorial value, be reasonably well written and be produced (published) at minimum cost to merge into its market niche with a decent profit for the producer.

Trade publishing is generally described as a business activity of concerns which publish ten or more author-written books a year for general distribution throughout the market. Conglomerates often encompass TV, magazines, newsletters and whatever, with their book publishing operation. A few houses produce hundreds of titles every year. Most trade-book publishers are much smaller. In the middle, between the self-publisher and trade houses are independent publishers. They purchase some books from outside authors, a few of their titles may be written by employees or the owner, and they manage production schedules ranging from two to ten books a year. This is my end of the business for several simple reasons: I'm never too busy to enjoy frequent vacations and the stress factor is approximately zero. Enough said.

Now it's your turn.

When you really have comfortable reasons to believe in a self-publishing project, ignore the nay-sayers and move on. You're more likely to be right than they will ever be. Besides, you have the momentum of enthusiasm which is the basis of some of the world's greatest money-making successes. You are well advised to plan positive and find yourself among those self-publishers who break even or make a bit of money. If you hit the jackpot, kick back, enjoy success, a fat bank account, then do another book.

Major money-making is possible, as a nearby talented self-publisher has proven. The lady came up with a great book appealing to adults as a gift for children. She did all the right things with distribution to bookstores, participation in author signings and all the media mailings she could make. The latter included sending out hundreds of books from which she received not one single review. One day she did the numbers and decided that she was working for peanuts, like netting 85 cents from a $19.95 book. Everyone else in the book trade distribution chain was making the money and the lady was not happy.

She no longer sells through trade channels. In two years she has moved $800,000 worth of books of which she retains about half the income after marketing and publishing costs have been paid. For her second book (as of 1999 she's done four) she increased the price by one dollar over the average of the highest priced competitive titles. She only sells to stores and through distributors when they send a check with the order, thereby eliminating delays in being paid or the possibility of never being paid. "After testing and trying them all, go for the market with the best dollar return," she told me late one evening.

So where does she market her books?

By reading area newspapers she finds fund raising events at which she can sell books and give the sponsors a small percentage. Plus direct selling at street fairs, seminars, church events and other happening at which there will be people. All her books are sold personally bearing a gold embossed sticker "First Edition. Signed by Author." And she has convinced more than one local self-publisher that "Authors make money lecturing...not as authors." $800,000 worth of her books sold in two years. Not bad for a self-publisher !

Publishing a printed book is a great business for the free-spirited. Despite electronic clutter of competition (like TV, the Internet, and whatever arrives tomorrow) books are likely to be with us for a long time. Besides, researchers may find your book a useful resource long after you're gone which is much better than only leaving a tombstone.

About This Book

The nitty-gritty of this chapter is that some rules will apply to give you the best shot at profiting from book publishing. In later chapters I'm going to tell you about the rules as I see them, explain what I have learned, and outline useful parameters affecting the business of which you plan to become a part. Some of the regimen is just plain dull, some a bit exciting and all of it based on experience, the sharing of which will improve your opportunities for success. At least I'll try to restrain your eagerness to repeat the same mistakes I've already paid for. By absorbing what I have learned, and doing all the careful planning early, you can proceed without the unnecessary distraction of worrying about doing it all wrong.

In conclusion, let me emphasize that I know what I'm doing in the book publishing field and the guide lines following are my sincere efforts to help you self-publish for profit. However, the suggested routines are not cast in concrete. Be free to change the sequence of steps to suit yourself. But, in all fairness, learn from my experience and be certain to thoughtfully consider the majority of basics described in the many chapters of this book. Giving them your best will maximize your potential for success.

There's always the question of peers. Who are in this business and what are they doing? From a recent survey, here's a few answers which may be useful as guidance.

Self publishers usually do one book and stop. A few move on to becoming independent publishers and emerge as genuine profit centers. This latter group publishes and keeps in print an average of about ten books. Earnings are in the mid-six-figure area and the owners work a full six-day business week. They're heavy in how-too, self-help and business-oriented titles. Those who do fiction usually specialize in poetry or books for children. Best of all, about two-thirds of small publishers work at home.

Successful Book Publishing

They report the costs of book production (1999) as from $500 to $3500 for a useful cover design, a mid-range of $75 an hour for book text-area design and about $10 an hour for someone to do page layouts. If perchance you wonder about the amount of time involved in book production, figure 70 to 75 working days for a non-fiction book and a bit less for fiction titles. Of this, estimate two days to design a book cover, eight days to edit a manuscript and at least three days to write a good news release and design the kit that should go with it. Release kits usually include the author's biography, a photo or two, a very well written news release and brief cover letter. All this could travel inside a quality folder containing a sample of your book's cover or color print of same.

The contents of *Self Publishing Made Easy"* are in a somewhat logical order that works well for me; although I must admit that I am often working on several tracks at the same time to keep production moving at reasonable speed. No matter how you or I do it, the beginning of a book is the explosive evidence of a great concept. I discuss this exciting inspiration point and suggest means of validation while briefly touching on the whole process of book publishing in the next chapter "Your Concept."

"Synopsis Preparation," the chapter which follows "Your Concept," will guide you through a slow-moving but demanding process to distill your best thinking. My simplistic approach is to accept the concept idea and springboard from that into designing a book appealing to the widest possible audience of potential buyers.

Because we're looking forward to your self-publishing project being profitable, the chapter following "Synopsis Preparation" is simply "The Competition." None of us wants to throw our time or efforts to the wind and this chapter directs you through a simple exercise of market research. That effort involves determining what's out there, how it is packaged, sold and, perhaps most importantly, how you could benefit from reviewing all the related books on bookseller shelves.

Eventually you will be facing the dollar cost of publishing a book I present "Stop or Go" as a pivot point for your decision about proceeding with a book or dropping the project. With perhaps the best argument for dropping an idea being that after inspecting the competition you may discover an even better theme to publish as your first project.

"Marry the Market" is a strange title for a succeeding chapter which relates to merging your interests firmly with the market and potential buyers of your title. Once you decide on those individuals most likely to buy, designing a book to meet their needs improves the potential for profit. In this regard, all bets are off if you are planning to publish a family history or autobiography for relatives. In this instance it will be easy to absorb the details of actually getting your book into print at low cost. Though you may skip my emphasis on making a profit there are benefits from the many suggestions for buying your printing services are reasonable cost.

The TOC, or "Working Table of Contents" chapter, is a vital keystone to self publishing. Consider it as the initial architectural design of your home. It expresses your objective and establishes a comfortable overview of what will be inside the walls. A TOC works the same way. It is an overview of the structure of your book and often the first-read page of those book shoppers seriously considering a book purchase.

Once the TOC is finalized I'll run you through the techniques of deciding on "Words Per Chapter." This is another budgeting area of book publishing. Here you decide on the desired amount of text in the book, parcel out percentages of size to individual chapters and in the doing establish flexible parameters for the amount of writing you will have to do to express your subject fully. My point is that there's little logic in overworking if a comfortable minimum will do the job.

"Writing to Fit" would be an unusual chapter in any book because it has nothing to do with the craft of writing. Instead I'm talking about the importance of word count. Like writing enough, then a little more to provide editing options, and never being faced with spending money to publish a book that's too long or short for its market niche at the booksellers.

The trauma of "First Reading" your manuscript can be greatly reduced, and easily switched to sheer pleasure, if you'll seriously consider my hints in this chapter. What to look for and what to ignore are as important as how to relax and totally enjoy the wonderful experience of your book's birthing.

It takes two people to edit text well and you have the opportunity to be both of them in "Copy Flow and Text Editing." I separate these two functions and explain the easy methods of successfully fine tuning the writing in your book.

"Drafts, Drafts, Drafts" is my way of not only emphasizing but insisting that you output your book, on your desktop printer, as many times as necessary. Then draft-print it at least once again for perfection.

Adjusting a computer to format printed book pages is easy to do once you find the appropriate instructions in the manual. You'll find that such program information merges well with my chapter on "Computer Settings" which lays out the benefits of carefully formatting a book during this important pre-press step in the self publishing process.

The Table of Contents and Index of every book are primary selling tools. In my chapter on "Front and Back Matter" you'll find many ways of creating these critical sections of your book.

The needful page by page adjustments of your book, after being desk-top printed in its ready-to-go-to-print book format, are easily accomplished. In my chapter on "Proofing To Print" are many things to look for, how to fix common publishing problems and methods for inserting photographs and art into the desired location on text pages without tearing the entire book into pieces.

Successful Book Publishing

With expense of book printing being about about 50% paper cost, my subsequent chapter on "Paper Stock Selection" leads you through the (be)wilderness of text paper stocks. From Bible to newsprint, thick to thin, expensive to cheap; they're all here for your decision as to their affect on book cost.

"Book Covers," the chapter after "Paper Stock," details the marketing importance of a superior book cover. Considering that spine and cover are the first thing a book-store shopper views, you may appreciate my emphasize on this important design stage of self publishing for success.

Because it's your money, and a profitable book provides more happiness than a loser, "The Best Printing Price" is one of my longest chapters. Here I discuss how to find a printer, obtain those important preliminary bids and clarification of technical terms contained in the resulting quotations.

Next up is "Evaluating Book Bids." This is a crucial chapter before ordering your book printed. Trade terms are discussed, the contract is clarified item by item with tricks and traps of the estimates disclosed for your inspection and decision. If you read only one chapter of *Self Publishing Made Easy* this should be it for the many details of deciding on the printer with whom to do business.

"Sending it Away for Printing" may seem to be superfluous guidance but there are many slips between the hand and mouth in ordering printing. Here are the final cautions and insurances for maintaining a fair printing price and a fast turn-around for the manufacturing and delivering your completed book.

While your book is wandering through a manufacturer's plant there are a number of productive things you can do. In "Very Good Busy Work" I line them up for your inspection and considered activity.

"Your Books Arrive" covers the nuts and bolts of book storage, critical first steps to initiate once books are on hand and suggestions about the best-ever productive distribution of those early arriving copies.

From now on its all about selling books to insure the most rapid return on investment. In "Marketing Your Books" are more ways to exchange books for money than you can use in a couple of years. Pick and choose those which fit your available time and personal pattern best.

The wholesale book trade of jobbers and distributors is somewhat complicated. I've done my best in "Distributors, Jobbers and You" to make it simple for you to go forward with successful moves onto the bookseller's shelves.

"Publicity (Print)" details an important half of the publicity farm. In this chapter you will find complete instructions on seeking publicity in newspapers, periodicals and magazines. Plus how to do it at lowest cost with the most productive results. Though publicity is work, it's an effort that pays off royally with increased book sales.

"Publicity (Radio/TV)" is the other half of the promotion opportunity world. Both radio and TV exposure are attainable by the self-publisher and here's how. Plus important details of continuing to encourage coverage and how best to make use of the extended potential of it all.

Hundreds of thousands of dollars have been gained by self publishers selling their book by hand and mouth. In "Sell Them Yourself" you'll learn why they did it and how you can utilize their techniques to your advantage.

"Money In The Bank" is an afterthought chapter. It was written after I realized we could use a bit of coverage on such small stuff as the best way to open a publisher's bank account, obtain charge cards and consider useful techniques for handling money at the lowest cost.

There's a bit of tongue-in-cheek in the chapter "Will You Become Rich?" because I believed it was important to express the good and the barely possible of self publishing. You'll find it all here with examples of great success as compared to reasons self-published books may be profitless or only break even much to the self-publisher's discouragement.

The "Glossary" is a wonderful collection of common terms in the book production business. It's worth reading carefully before you talk to a printer's customer representative. With such background you are much better equipped to know precisely what they're talking about and how technicalities affect book prices on the bookseller's shelves. And, perhaps best of all, you'll have good material to sound professional and knowledgeable when talking with printer reps.

The "References" section is an important portion of this book. Here you will find current addresses of many supportive resources for self-publishing entrepreneurs, authors and publishers.

I've tried to create a fat useful "Index" to make this book easier to use. Though there's hundreds of entries, no doubt you will wish for a few that should have been included. Let me know what they are and I'll insert them on the next printing of *Self Publishing Made Easy*.

Meanwhile let's move on into the wonderful field of refining your concept of a book and initiate a successful self-publishing program.

Your Concept

Let's begin at the beginning with your idea for a book; and if by chance you've started to write it: Stop Now !

Put that manuscript safely away in a place you'll not remember too easily for a long time. In short don't even think about an incomplete book until you fully consider what follows in this chapter, wherein I'm going to discuss your basic idea or concept and suggest successful methods of fine-tuning it for more profitable fruition. The best tuning I know about is a combination of brainstorming and planning. Afterward writing will flow with ease and you'll record thoughts you didn't even know you had and a few you just as soon forget.

Your Concept

Validation of a concept begins with accepting the overwhelming desire to share your book idea with others. From them you'll probably receive one of three responses.

Nay-sayers do their thing with "Are you kidding? No one will ever buy a book about that."

In the mid-range are those of limited awareness who come back with "Oh, that's very interesting. By the way, I must tell you that it may snow/rain/freeze tomorrow."

What may be be least helpful of all are those who offer thoughtless support. They care so much about you as a person that anything you come up with, such as a one-man submarine trip to Hawaii or rabbit hunting on Mars, sounds good to them. "What a marvelous idea," they'll gush. "I do want a copy when you publish it." In your politic heart you know they've not bought a book in the past ten years.

When you finally get a live one, who really likes books, inquires about the title, is genuinely interested in details of the subject matter, number of pages and marketing plans; listen up. Their questions will be more than helpful by forcing you to formulate thoughtful answers. Talk it through with them and listen carefully. Then merge their comments and questions with your concurrent thoughts on treatment, book size, covers, method of selling and everything else that surfaces during the conversation. This is a reasonable example of productive brainstorming that is to your advantage.

Your Concept

Continue talking about your book concept for not less than one full week of face to face conversation with every person who will listen; including the friendly supermarket check-out girl, bank teller and waitress. What you're seeking is the answer for two questions. "Who needs it?" and "What will they do with the book and why?" Everything goes. If you're lucky one of your conversationalists may have that very special suggestion to make you wealthy.

Here's an example of how a clever twist on an old subject paid off. The original concept was a book for expectant parents which would tell them how to handle the nine-month project. The clever twist was to provide the information in a month-to-month format matching the gestation period. Neat idea. So neat that by late 1998 the authors were reported to have sold nearly five million (5,000,000) copies of *What to Expect When You're Expecting.* Did they take a vacation? No way. They produced three related titles which sell well.

Now here's another surprise for you.

During your week of conversations about your book concept please don't write anything down or you will tend to formalize the entire project. Let thoughts and valuable comments rattle around between your ears. The very best suggestions will be retained and come to the surface when you really need them later, while moving forward into successful book publishing.

Continue thinking "Book and People" within every bit of space and time. Like making a baby, this is the fun part of conception. Enjoy it while you can.

Your Concept

Hard work, in this instance "writing," lies ahead in the more than nine-months needed to bring your little rascal to market.

Enjoy fantasizing about all the wild and wonderful places in which to sell your book. How much advertising? What media would you like? Cost? Where do you think publicity could be successful? Which social or service clubs would like to hear you speak about your self-published book? Who should wholesale and distribute your book to the trade and how could they help you market it? Think dirty. Think sales. This mind-game is where the overall concept develops and your time is well invested because no money is spent nor stress involved.

Most important: If you would be profitable be sure you have repeatedly questioned yourself and everyone else about the twins: "Who needs my book and Why?"

It's a warm fuzzy to park the resulting collection of stimulating thoughts in the brain cells. No obligation is involved and neither is stress. So think more. Then think about it all over again while keeping in mind all you need do at this stage of the game is fantasize. To repeat, perchance you missed it, write nothing down for that will happen in the next chapter. Otherwise you may consider such current notes of undue importance. Right now they're not.

Free association is the name of the game in bootstrapping a good book concept into a brilliant publishing project. It's a simple information gathering technique that reduces clutter and makes analysis easier. Everything is possible at this stage and there are no limits. When you brainstorm, all is doable. Encompass your best and if you question merits of this approach to self-publishing, please consider the following true story.

Some years ago, in the midwest, a retired gentleman built a hobby-horse for his grandson. For those of you much younger, a hobby horse is basically an old broom stick to which the wooden cutout of a horse's head is attached at one end. The child straddles the horse-stick and jumps and prances with imagination and fantasy. Neat fun. No batteries to wear out and it is easily parked behind the family home's kitchen door.

Friends saw this first "horse" and asked if he would make others for their children. Soon the gentleman was busy making hobby horses. Being of a curious nature he began to research the history of this delightful toy and became a highly regarded historian. As he learned, and built other hobby horses, his expertise developed into part-time consulting as an appraiser of antique hobby horses. You have no doubt guessed that he eventually published a successful book about hobby horses. Need more? A happy man doing what he enjoys. A profitable book on a most unlikely subject. And a national reputation. We should do so well from enjoying a hobby and building a career.

That is all I'm asking you to do in this early chapter of *Self-Publishing Made Easy*. Think about the

Your Concept

book you want to write. And keep on thinking about it until you bore yourself silly. This this will make it much easier to produce a successful book and is the most productive fun you will have in the publishing field.

Synopsis Preparation

In this chapter, you will have an opportunity to write something. The catch being; it must not only be very, very, good but it is not likely to ever be published.

During the following suggested seven days of critical work you are being asked to force yourself to distill every drop of creative juices into a thoughtful outline of a book. Everything in the synopsis you are going to write will be modified and polished day after day by the earlier brainstorming discussions you held with others about the project's concept. On conclusion you will know precisely what you want to write about, for the specific audience you plan to reach, and be better prepared to do so in a comprehensive fashion. In short, you'll have your act together.

Self Publishing Made Easy

Synopsis Preparation

While creating this one-page briefing you can nurture, then refine, all those wonderful ideas that floated about during the brainstorming sessions recommended in the previous chapter. Those same good thoughts will now emerge and interact while you're working your way through initial planning stages of your book publishing program. Because nothing was supposed to be written, and you were thinking only good thoughts about a book, the brain cells were also fussing with possible titles which we'll use in a few moments.

Though up to now you've spent no money, that changes here because I'm going to send you shopping.

Buy a brand-new 8-1/2 by 14-inch yellow legal pad and a brand new pen that fits your fingers perfectly. Why new? Because that expenditure represents your commitment to the project. Pad and pen are tangible evidence of your desire to publish a better than average book. Besides, as related to printing a book, the price of such tools is insignificant.

Select the nearest upcoming week offering an hour or so that can be scheduled about the same time for seven days. Privacy is important even if you have to drive to a public recreation site, park, beach, mountain top or just curb-side a few blocks away to evade telephone, kids, TV or whatever. For sure, now's the time you deserve peace and quiet to let a treasure trove of "book" thoughts tumble out onto that non-judgmental pad of yellow sheets.

Self Publishing Made Easy

Synopsis Preparation

Date and time the first sheet at the top and write down every working title you have thought of. For this book, at first it was just *Publishing*. You can add or modify title suggestions as you travel in subsequent months, as I did four times. For now we're only flushing possible titles from the brain cells to better focus on the next clean page where I want you to write a one-page synopsis of your proposed book. To better define this project please consider the dictionary definition of a synopsis: "A condensed statement or outline (as of narrative or treatise)."

That's it. The synopsis you are writing is nothing more and nothing less. Worst of all, you are absolutely limited to one side of one sheet of yellow paper on which to lay your precious thoughts. The synopsis should be handwritten no matter how badly you scribble for there's demonstrated value in going directly from the brain to the pen. Thinking does not flow too freely through a keyboard and your best brain power should be represented in the synopsis, not electronic dilutions.

Be that as it may. One sheet. Write as large or as small as you wish. (Should you come up with neat additional title thoughts, they go on the top sheet.) Corrections or additions to the synopsis should be written on that lonely second sheet; between the lines, sideways, slaunchways or upside down because this is an "everything goes" experience. One sheet of paper, one side, one session during one day's time frame.

Self Publishing Made Easy

Synopsis Preparation

And no cheating allowed.

So simple it's frightening. More difficult than these simple words may make it appear. A useful synopsis of your book is now on the way.

The next day, at more or less the proximate time, in a writing site of peace and quiet, read what you wrote yesterday.

Yuk?

But it's the most valuable beginning you will ever make and one you'll value for a long time to come.

After reviewing the pad's first synopsis sheet· keep it safe by folding it back over the top binding. Date and time the second clean sheet. Rewrite the synopsis a second time. Change as you wish. Write small or large, in every direction. But remember; only one second sheet, on one side of the paper, a better description of your proposed book. If you upchuck any new titles add them to the title-only sheet.

On the next day re-read the second synopsis and be happy with the neat feeling of "Hey...this is a bit better."

With that feat of self-encouragement rewrite the second synopsis a third time. Longer, shorter, smaller, larger, new material in, old material out, probably fewer deletions and kitty-cornered additions. But don't forget: One side of one sheet, no more, no less. As a reminder, here again is the dictionary definition of synopsis: "A condensed statement or outline (as of narrative or treatise)."

Self Publishing Made Easy

Synopsis Preparation

While it may seem maddening, on the fourth day review epic three and rewrite your concept synopsis a fourth time. Date, time, one sheet, one side, etc.

Then do it all over again, in a peaceful place, the fifth time. One sheet, one side.

"A condensed statement or outline (as of narrative or treatise)." is what you are continuing to create. It's a very short form of your entire book. What the book is all about, how it gets there and something of its values for a reader. Anyone reading this fifth day's synopsis should gain a fairly clear idea of what your self-publishing project is all about. The rock and the hard place is that if you can't explain your book concept on one (legal size) sheet of paper it's not likely you will ever explain it well in 300 pages of a costly-to-print book.

The sixth day is slightly different. It begins with date and time at the top of the blank sheet. Then select your favorite "working title" to be written next to date and time as a focal point. The difference is that on this go-around you should very carefully review the synopsis from the fifth day and rewrite it at your most skillful best on the sixth sheet. In short, edit Number Five and write Number Six with every bit of talent you can muster. Polish paragraphs well and then polish every phrase, word, comma and period to support the working title you like best.

Be happy. The next day's synopsis, Number Seven, is near and it's the last one.

Self Publishing Made Easy

Synopsis Preparation

Date, time and title this important final seventh sheet. Review synopsis Number Six and rewrite it as Number Seven to absolute perfection that fits on one side of a sheet of the legal pad. When this is finished it's time to type or computer input the handwritten material from the seventh sheet so you can reproduce it as printed hard-copies for use later on.

There's little question but what this seven-day marathon seems like strong medicine for a short description of a book you plan to publish. Trouble it may be but it's a valuable money-saving trouble in this field of publishing. The seven days have made your future steps to success that much easier. Should you doubt my comment, imagine trying to build a new house without first picturing what form the structure should present to the eye. In home building this is called the design phase. For your book it's creating a synopsis from which you're going to design and build a complete book.

Your synopsis, as printed out, is the bed and breakfast of communication for your book. With synopsis in hand you can do market research, build the book's framework, enhance that with writing skills and subject knowledge then successfully complete a self-publishing project that really communicates.

I'm presenting this now as one of several ways to make your writing much easier than ever before. Not only will you have a concise concept but you will be comfortable in filling the space available. And you'll

Self Publishing Made Easy

Synopsis Preparation

soon discover that an estimate of the percentage of space and words per chapter is just about right for everything you can think of that belongs in that specific chapter. This works though you didn't worry too much about available space while writing.

Of equal importance: After you read the next chapter about your competition you can intelligently decide to proceed, or to drop the project at this stage. What I have been doing is preparing you to dedicate yourself to doing a book. Not just any book, but your book. Or, as an alternative, have prepared you to save bundles of time and dollars by not venturing into an expensive self-publishing project which revolves around a mystic concept you are unable to articulate on one simple sheet of yellow paper.

The Competition

With all that good "Synopsis" work behind us, and I do consider it work having formed a goodly number of profitable books in that precise fashion, we move on. Our upcoming good use of that seventh day of rewriting will be to validate the synopsis with market research techniques outlined in this chapter on checking out the competition.

These techniques are preliminary to actually writing your book because you are well advised to have an objective (buyer) for your writing. Such an objective is the sensible alternative to a basic mistake of many self-publishers. They often write and publish a expensive book before determining if there is anyone out there to buy it. As a symbolic example, the book you are now reading is considerably different than one encouraging your involvement with "Self-Publishing for the Fun of It," a mistake often made. The difference being that I'm going to detail opportunities to make bankable money from your book.

Reviewing the competition is trade-smart. Major publishers frequently do market research across a broad spectrum of buyer interests before they have a specific book subject, title or author in mind. On observing an opening in a market area, or on the heels of another publisher's successful title, they order a book written for that observed market niche. Consider such publishing as similar to the way you and I would order hotcakes for breakfast. That is not, in my opinion, the best method for self-publishers who usually have only one area of expertise. In self-publishing the author/publisher is the only one who knows what he/she wants to write about. With that expertise as the foundation, what is learned by researching a specific project is likely to improve the benefits of the recently completed "Concept" brainstorming and what you have written in the synopsis. Accordingly, market research results usually culminate in one of three common areas: One, it's a bum idea for a book. Two, it's the world's greatest idea. Three, there's an even better way to present the same theme. By doing basic market research outlined in this chapter you can estimate economic/profit values of a self-publishing project and establish its potential for success or failure.

The short form of all this is best said as "Look before you leap."

The Competition

As a contrary continuum, I work best by developing my ideas to their fullest without outside influence. This means I do my creative uninhibited best, instead of compromising with or meeting the needs of others, during the concept-synopsis stage. Certainly this is not the advice given given you in the "Concept" chapter when I suggested talking "book" with others. This is just the way I operate. It does not change my recommendation to you and emphasizes the obvious: There's more than one way to skin a cat. The compromising of my very personal concept and synopsis comes on strong during subsequent market research. That's when I begin modifying the planned book to meet potential-reader comments and observed market needs. In this respect, I've never been reluctant to change or abandon a project book when I could not observe a profitable customer base into which it might be sold.

None of the above marketing discussion applies to self-publishing an autobiography or family history, should those areas be your interest. You could easily skip the rest of this chapter as it does not relate to such projects which are rarely done with a profit motive in the prospective publisher's mind.

Be that as it may. The methods in this guidebook work for me. What works for you is best for you. Perchance you're a bit lost as to how to effectively proceed, it's easy to follow my lead and, at least, you'll end up with a marketable book which may make some money over and above its production cost.

The Competition

So let's go to work on the money side of self publishing a book to fit the most profitable market.

With synopsis firmly in mind, small note pad and pen in hand, visit every nearby bookstore and inspect available publications in your proposed field of endeavor. Same visit suggestion applies to reference shelves of the nearest public library. In addition the library's magazine section is a fine source of information about similar books that may be advertised or reviewed in periodicals with related editorial matter. Mail-order catalogue offers and book advertisements in collateral publications not specific to your theme provide a good background about potential competitors and shoppers likely to consider the purchase of your may-be published book.

There's a small chart on the next page from which to make a dozen or so copies. Your local copy shop, or desktop scanner, can upsize it to full letter size. If you cover the right side displaying my data, with a piece of white paper when you copy, there will be room for your notes in place of the examples I have included. The multiple copies will be handy as a means of logging a very useful record of important factors found in competitive books. We will consider and make use of this data while continuing to explore the self-publishing process as related to your personal objectives.

The Competition

Chart for Book Inspection

Title	*Self-Publishing Made Easy*
Pub/(C) Date	Copyright 1999 William Carroll
Size Inches	6- by 9-inches
Chapters	32
Pages	280+
Lines Per Page	30
Words Per Line	9.6
Type Size	12 pt.
Paper Stock: Thin, Med, Thick	Medium
Price	25.00
Ten-Foot Cover: Y or N	Yes
Cover Art/Photo/Text/Color/B&W	Art/PMS Colors
Text Pages: Art/Photos/Tables/	Tables
Color Pages: Y or N	No
References: Y or N	Yes
Index: Y or N	Yes
Back cover description	Contents Detailed
Pitches other books or this book?	This book
Inside cover material	Yes
Pitches other books or this book?	
Overall Impression, Package feel.	Quality / Medium
Shelved in what classification?	Writing/Authorship

The Competition

While you're inspecting a bookseller's stock of competitive titles, use copies of the chart for your report on each book's overall size, paper stock, size of text, use of drawings (with big being considered better) and use of photography. Full color pages are great but expensive enough to be worth noting if their use is common in your subject field. When most comparable books contain color, you should budget many, many, dollars to become equal. Or you could be home free with the lower cost production of using black and white photographs, drawings or none of the above.

The date of publication is useful. If most books are old, there could well be be room for a new title. Take plenty of time to review long-ago titles. You may find a wealth of things you could do better or augment with more current information and in the doing make your book an outstanding success.

If most of the books are new, think again as the market niche and subject matter could be overfed.

A "ten-foot cover" is very important. Of the new and used books that you inspect, decide how many of them have a cover that carries a positive message to a shopper standing ten feet away? A very important point if the book is displayed cover out. Shoppers must be able to read the title quickly and, hopefully, want to stop for an inspection as they trudge past row after row of books. An outstanding cover seduces casual shoppers into an "open the book" mode. A nondescript cover is seldom noticed. You'll find examples of both.

The Competition

Counting the approximate number of words in competitive books is easy. Count words in ten lines. Move the decimal point left for words per line (87 words in ten lines is 8.7 words per line). Multiply words per line by the number of lines per full typical page and that answer by number of pages in the book. Example: 8.7 Words per line with 30 lines per page is 261 words which in a 100-page book totals 26,100 words for the entire book. During in-store market research, it's best to merely note words per line, lines per page and number of pages. Save the heavy math for homework and coffee a bit later.

If you're not sure about type sizes, before you leave home adjust your computer program to print out a few lines of any text in 8-point, 10-point, and 12-point size. Choose a type that is something like that used in your local newspaper. Specific sizes are selectable from your publishing or word processing program. When you inspect the competition you'll be able to quickly make an eyeball comparison of the size type used. This knowledge becomes very important in your project when, later on, size and cost of the proposed book requires important ajustment decisions.

Flip (fan) the pages rapidly of a number of peripheral books which somewhat relate to your project. How are they formatted? Wide margins or narrow? Photography, drawings or text only? Index, references or neither? Your overall eyeball impression is the valuable question worth answering and recording. You are sure to find some books that appear immensely difficult to view. Others will invite you to buy them "Right now" and read them soonest. Why peripheral books? Because they are books which could give you ideas from slightly outside your field, which ideas may add freshness or impressive useful differences to your niche project.

In addition, while inspecting what is current in your specific area of interest, as time permits talk with the bookstore owner or clerks to solicit their opinion of your plans. Booksellers are great people and often provide keys to success for self-publishers by suggesting niche areas in need of your title. They may even save you money by naming ten other books in your concept area: None of which is selling well enough to encourage another of the same theme.

Of course it's worth keeping in mind that booksellers consider all author/publishers a bit mad. However, they know the market best and can offer valuable good and bad input. If they support your project it indicates that you are probably in the right track. If they universally frown on it, changes may be necessary. Yes; back to seven more days of new synopsis preparation. Or they may recommend modifications you would have made yourself had you thought of them. Best of all, with friendly professionals, there's no need to be defensive about your book or you could turn off their helpful input.

The more stores you visit, the better to inquire about sale in your subject area. If the subject is dead in its tracks, stop! If slow, plan carefully. Or hurry up.

The Competition

Also determine, with the shop owner's help, the shelf category in which he or she believes your book should be displayed. Booksellers and clerks will make use of your designation (Accounting, Regional Interest, Diets, etc.) off the back cover near the UPC code (more later on this) for guidance to new employees restocking shelves in the area most supportive of your theme.

In short, dredge up a "feeling" response for your book which impression you can reflect on as you travel from store to store. Does the subject continue to "feel good" or are the vibes depressing. Keep in mind that even with bad vibes it is your book and a reasonable number of "against the odds" books have successfully become profitable despite negative opinions and poor reviews. In this connection you may recall that earlier bit about the "momentum of enthusiasm" which has created the best of successes. Momentum is really important and can work to your advantage if such support for enthusiasm is not misunderstood stubbornness.

Even if they seem expensive, buy a copy of one or two best-liked books in the field in which you propose to publish. They will be excellent guides to number of pages and the price bracket impacting your concept of how your book should be designed. Address special attention to recommended books you feel good about from what you read or from page layout and illustrations. If there's a used-book retailer in the area your research dollars can purchase a wider collection of titles that relate (even remotely) to your topic. Later, at home, fill in your charts for used book inspection and evaluate each title for appeal to the casual browser/shopper who has just taken one or more off the shelf. Position yourself as a reader who knows little of the subject, then re-position yourself as the knowledgeable reader, and finally consider the competition's appeal to the specific group of readers you propose to reach.

The big question being, are you duplicating a number of books already on the market? There's nothing wrong with that as long as what you are planning has a great title and fresh/better approach to the subject. Otherwise slavish duplication could be sheer financial disaster.

While this seems like much ado, keep in mind that the foregoing market research enhances your potential for financial success from publication of the book. Research may also save you from the dollar drain of owning a garage full of identical Christmas presents guaranteed to last during the next 200 years. For sure, should you find five or ten titles that are near duplicates of your project, self-publishing a similar book is likely to be of doubtful value. Should there be but one or two titles, room for another and better book would seem to exist and you may decide to consider moving forward.

After booksellers, the second-best source of marketing information is a publication known as *Books In Print*. It's a humongous affair in book form and much more usable on the computer screen. With it you can learn what else has been published in the field you intend to enter. Pages, price and year of publication are your key factors. Should all the books be old, there could be room for a new one. The reverse situation, of many new title releases, calls for serious reconsideration of your plans to invest money in printed paper. And, as I mentioned previously, spend a bit of extra time to wander through related fields. While planning a book about furniture; look for titles on upholstery, wood finishing, home decorating, etc. You may be surprised to find good reasons to modify your synopsis or find equally valid reasons to leave it completely alone and charge ahead.

Worry not about titles similar to those on your title list. Titles are not copyrighted. You'll often find a number of books with near identical titles separated only by different authors or publishers. Along this route of market research you may come up with additional draft (temporary) titles for your book. Anytime is right to record the latest and keep right on recording every one that comes to mind. The longer a list the better, when it comes time to adopt the best.

Which brings me to an important point. Think dirty about a title for your book. As you have now learned, books are indexed somewhat in the fashion of the telephone book's business pages. Should a book be "How to Design, Engineer and Build Wheelbarrows" it's indexing is a marketing problem. Will it be found under "How To,", "Design" or "Engineer?" If you wanted to find a book about wheelbarrows, would you look under such classifications? Revise that title to read "Wheelbarrow Design, Engineering and Construction" and potential buyers will find the book where it belongs: Under "W" for "Wheelbarrows."

It is almost a certainty that some of the books you found shelved in stores were poorly titled and presented covers that were hard to decipher from a distance. Hopefully you found other books that were gems of clarity in displaying their worth. Take your pick as to how you wish to design your package. Good covers and clever titles sell books because they encourage potential buyers to open pages. Plan ahead. Upgrade your potential for success from "maybe" to "likely" by spending adequate time learning all you can about what is on the market and how it is presented.

Here's what this chapter was all about. Being profitable and making money. If you now feel better prepared, move on; unless you're discouraged and would like to just trash the whole self-publishing idea, start over with a better concept or go to a movie. It's self-serving on my part but you may be ahead of the game to continue reading *Self-Publishing Made Easy* and learn more about the great, good, and the awful of this wonderful publishing business. To help you further, in the next chapter we'll slow a bit to reflect on whether or not to take the plunge toward actually completing or writing, designing, and paying good money to print and publish a book.

Stop or Go ?

It's a jungle out there in the book business.

About 60 percent of all book sale's dollars fatten the bank accounts of a half-dozen huge publishing houses. Best estimates are that 60 to 70 percent of their new titles lose money, or barely break even and give their editors heartburn. One of three hard-bound books is sold to a library. If you wonder about mass-market paperbacks, the news is equally grim. As of 1999, a trade paperback from a major publisher had to sell about 15,000 copies to recover costs.

Worst of all, one in five Americans is functionally illiterate and wouldn't read a book if you gave it to them.

Stop or Go ?

On the positive side; these situations, which are considered problems to the majors, expose a wealth of opportunity for the minors. Which minors certainly include self-publishers where innovative books are birthed and unexpected best-sellers herald the emergence of fine new authors. Without the huge overhead of big trade houses, a small publisher or self-publisher can produce a truly different book at the lowest possible cost. This price advantage is a real plus when facing competitive titles from major publishing houses. Accordingly, please don't let my presentation of both sides of the publishing business be discouraging. Books will be with us for a long time and many small publishers will make a lot of money supplying information to those who read.

It's your decision, to Stop or Go. This very brief chapter is inserted here to give you a bit of breathing time before proceeding to create a Table of Contents (TOC) which is the emotional commitment to spend real money while creating and publishing a book.

If you need something to do, while making the Stop/Go decision, and on the premise that you may proceed, we're going out for preliminary printing bids on a book you have yet to begin or complete. The logic is simple. You are planning the production of something that could be profitable. This emphasizes that you should write your book to a size comparable to competition. As well as have a useful idea if you can freely afford its considerable production cost before you waste a lot of time and enthusiasm in said writing.

Stop or Go ?

What we need now is to prepare a Preliminary Request for Quotation (Preliminary RFQ) which should be sent to a half dozen or so book printers. You'll find such printing resources in the "References" section at the back of this book. Our purpose is only to obtain a range of costs for producing a book similar to the competition. Have your local copy shop upsize the form from a following page to about letter size. Run off a couple of copies. Use the best-liked book of those you purchased as a sample. Detail it completely, including the overall size and page count, on a single form. In this book's chapter, "The Best Printing Price," are detailed instructions on filling in a preliminary bid form and what the various terms mean. Should you be unsure of any specification it is useful to leave the entry point blank. Across the top is the word "Preliminary" for guidance to the printer's estimators and hold the door open for serious negotiations later.

Use a copy machine to duplicate the filled-in form, a copy of which should be sent to each book production house. To each form you plan mailing, attach a clipping from the cover, and full page samples of the text paper of your best-liked competitive book. This gives the printer specific samples of stock to bid with. Also add a note or letter requesting samples of the printers "in-house" text paper in 50# and 60# weights, a sample of any book they have produced which is similar to your specifications and the business card of a representative. The latter is very important. Later on you may need a real live person to talk with

Stop or Go ?

instead of never-ending voice-mail codes and recorded messages explaining your importance to them. The copy of a preliminary bid form follows on the next page.

It will take a bit of time for the preliminary bid requests to come back so, in the interests of efficiency, let's develop an understanding of market position. This positioning is broadly defined as the development of parameters for a book package that merges seamlessly into the market niche you plan to reach. We've already discussed and learned about our objective which is the potential buyer. Now we're going to focus on publishing what you believe that specific buyer wants.

Stop or Go ?

Preliminary Bid Request

Name...

Company.......................................

Address..

City, State ZIP.............................

I need a quotation on the following

not later than

....

Please quote a quantity of ....

and additional.............................

Trim size of my book is...............

My page count is.........................

Text copy will be provided as:

      Camera Ready Copy

      Digital Files

        MAC   Dos/Windows

There are...........pictures

(halftones) to print in text.

The ink color of the text is

      Black throughout...........

      Or this color....................

The paper stock for my text is:

      50# 60# 70#

      Coated   Gloss   Matte

      Other................................

The color of the text paper is:

      White..............................

      Natural...........................

Cover/Dust jacket as:

      Camera ready copy

      Composite film w/proof

      Digital Files

          Mac   Dos/Windows

Colors for cover or jacket:

      4-Color Process (CMYK)

      Black plus......PMS colors.

Soft Cover binding style:

Perfect bound

      Notch bind

      Sew wrap

      Spiral wire

Cover stock to use:

      10 pt. C1S 12 pt. C1S

Cover finish:

      Laminate: Gloss Matte

      UV Coating

Hard Cover binding style:

      Adhesive Case

      Smyth Case

      Notch Case

Stamping: Foil color..................

      Front Spine Back

Shrink wrap books: Yes/No

Ship Books to City/State/ZIP

Marry The Market

Please read on for the good stuff to come, though it
may continue confusing that we are so early concerned
about selling a book yet to be written or completed. By
this time you have a far greater than average
knowledge about what is, and is not, available to
bookbuyers who may or may not be in need of your
book. Accordingly it is vitally important in the
publishing process that you design a product to fit that
specific market. Which designing phase is a totally
different task as compared to promoting or marketing
a printed book, a subject I'll cover in detail after your
completed books are on hand.

Marry The Market

Following are a number of vital elements in a useful fit-the-market plan in which you'll be busy marshaling troops to impress the very important bookdealer/distributor group, media and buyers. This is a tall order which should begin with thinking about a budget which includes spending money to give your book its initial momentum. As much as one-dollar a book to begin with or whatever less proves to be effective. Then consider the importance of product presentation. For your cover think about emphasizing the book's contents, author, quality of publication or whatever you can sincerely pitch as of prime selling importance. We'll get into cover design details later on in that specific chapter. All of which has to fit the audience you perceive as the most financially rewarding to approach.

As a reminder, if your self-publishing interest is an autobiography, "prestige" or "memory" book, do as you wish. The basics of merging into the market, in this chapter, would not apply. All you need do with such a prestige project is accept orders from relatives, collect their money first, publish in a lush format, write big checks and ship promptly. For this package, profit is moot, though cost-reducing techniques I'll outline in this book could be helpful. For other readers we're heading for production of a book that makes money on the open market.

An overview of the book trade involves everything you do as a self-publisher. Your book must meet trade standards for size and finish in a first-class manner or it simply won't sell. One or more distributors are important to establish and maintain a profitable volume of sales. They must be supported by your publicity and sales promotion efforts which are the key to book movement from publisher to buyer. These factors and selections should mesh in a viable form or you'll be among the losers in the field of self publishing entrepreneurship.

I can't say it often enough. Early planning is the key to building a satisfactory house and enjoyable profits from the book business.

Winners have their act together. Large and small publishing houses establish a fix on the specific book they intend to attract the greatest number of potential buyers. Successful self-publishers often have a very special way in which to satisfy the niche need of a reasonable number of potential buyers. Self publishers who best create a unique or skillfully updated book and position their publicity campaign to establish an image of responsible authenticity make the most money. Which is another value of preplanning and doing market research before spending printing dollars.

I'll present a collection of marketing tools in later chapters. Nevertheless near the project's beginning, you are well advised to be worrying up a storm while thinking "book sales" for every one of your future letters, brochures, direct mail pieces and publicity efforts. Merge them all in this planning while keeping them separate and powerful in the later doing.

Marry The Market

A simple example of preplanning lies in selecting the name of your publishing house. A new book published by Mary Smith is far less impressive than the identical book from Parkwood Press. Same book, same author, same publisher but different company name. If a choice existed, which book do you believe the bookseller or shopper would consider to be from the most reputable source?

Fear not, this often ignored factor is more logical than you may believe as any veteran publisher could tell you. With use of the research we've done, where books meet the bucks, you are far better prepared to market a salable (profitable) book as Parkwood Press than as Mary Smith. Besides, you will soon have the knowledge to specify a commercial package in terms of size, page count and price. Add the synopsis and merge these four vital factors to produce a focused book. Compare this to the financial risk of dumping a random collection of thoughts on paper while hoping someone will buy your output with which to pass the time of day or build a fire.

Let's run that by you again.

In the chapter on "Concepts," I encouraged you to do your best free thinking about the entire package. In effect, this stuffed your brain with more ideas than could be used in a decade. In the "Synopsis" chapter you were involved with writing the Who, Why, What, When, Where and How of your book. That one page synopsis told the entire story because you forced yourself to distill the best of your concepts into a clear and concise presentation. You were sent into book stores to learn about the competition, seek the guidance of owners and clerks then bulwark everything you previously did with their concepts and responses to your ideas. Somewhere along this line of thought plug into your planning the point that 80 percent of bookstore sales are to women and that mail-order sales are best made to very specific niche markets in which you create an "expert" image.

In effect, you are being requested to work hard to design and engineer the book you're soon to be involved with in both the building and paying for.

All the preceding is useful background for market planning which involves how you intend to sell the book: At your lectures, through mail-order advertising programs, local booksellers, jobber/distributor services to local and national retailers, or by means of the dozens of niche sales methods which can sometimes be very successful. Every one of these factors gives us cause to learn more of who actually accounts for the sale of books. Not only is the story you want to tell important but its place at booksellers is critical .

A few years ago there was a detailed report on the subject of where book sales are made. The next-page list speaks for itself. Is there any question as to where the major markets are? And these figures do not reflect the marketing of books on the internet where sales have increased dramatically.

Chain bookstores	25% of all books sold.	
Independents	21%	"
Book Clubs	18%	"
Discount Stores	8%	"
Warehouse Stores	6%	"
Used Book Stores	4%	"
Food/Drug Stores	4%	"
Other/Misc.	10%	"

Back to designing your profitable book. Here's a few odd-ball points to consider at this time.

A book copyrighted, dated and sold in December is one year old a month later in January. That same 13-month book is two years old the subsequent January. Booksellers and public alike tend to favor buying current books which means that a book two years old is not "fresh." Despite the quality of its contents, your title could drop out of the market because of a numeric age not really related to the true number of months it has been exposed to buyers. This copyright timing somewhat relates to when book stores restock. For summer selling they usually order for delivery of new stock in the March/April period. New titles preceding December holidays are usually ordered in the preceding August/September buying period.

So what's best? From my point of view one procedure is to release a book very early in the year to match the summer browser's market and (hopefully) nest on every bookseller's shelf all the way through December gift buying. Or print during the last quarter of the year, copyright it as of the first day of the next year, and after that date release it for sale. It will, because of the copyright date, be a "fresh" book for a full twelve months and can surf both summer and holiday sales waves. The caveat being that if you sell any books before the first day of the copyright, this procedure is not acceptable. Jumping the gun won't pay off. The true copyright date is the day you sold those few copies to friends. I strongly recommend that you read the Copyright regulations closely on this one. An information brochure and set of registry forms is available at no charge from the Copyright Office, Library of Congress, Washington, D.C. 20559.

All of which says: Plan production and on-sale date of your book to ride the book-market's business waves for maximum success. Which comment includes the need to preplan mail-order advertising. Magazines and newspapers have widely different "lead times" which merit serious consideration to make certain your book's advertising appears during the most effective selling period. A publication's "ad rep" can give you an accurate fix on lead times and may be willing to guide you into supportive special-theme issues and the best selling season for your book's niche market.

Mail-order sales generally follow the same trends as the retail book trade. If your book is going to be sold by mail, plan on sizing it to fit a protective container light enough to ship for minimum postage. Archive the formatted book on a computer disk so you can redo a successful title for newly expanded distribution to the trade (booksellers) as a second printing. Lecture book sales are in any book format and size, anytime you can get them, and I'll detail this special market a bit further on.

All of this worrying material is presented here for a single purpose. That is to submit to you, the author/publisher, the importance of preplanning a realistic and professional schedule of writing, production, printing and selling your self-published book. A simple schedule will do its part to prevent the enormous disappointment of publishing a great book only to be told, "Sorry, but we're not buying again for three or four months...it's our selling season now...not our buying time...the season for selling this title has passed."

That's as discouraging as the world ever becomes.

Think sales and think dollars in a fat bank account as you continue to modify preplanning for self-publishing success. Nothing here is cast in concrete. You should, and hopefully will, plan the self-publishing project again and again until you have firmed a comprehensive package of book size, format, best market target, writing, production and printing. It is right here, in these early stages of development, where you can most easily adjust everything from concept, quality, copies to print and price, at the simple stroke of a handy pen or pencil.

Such fine-tuning, as matched to your synopsis, is the foundation area of profitable authorship.

Working Table of Contents

After the fussing presented in my previous concerns, it's now time to begin establishing a sequence of chapters. This requires a working Table of Contents (TOC) with which to organize the text of your projected book so it flows logically from one subject area to another. What we're doing is simply drafting a TOC of one-line descriptions of your conception of what should be in each chapter to tell the book's story best.

To make life easier, here's a method that works well for me. With the synopsis as a foundation, record every identifiable chapter you find in the synopsis by writing a single line explaining what that specific chapter will report. Worry not about correctness of the sequence with this list of one-liners. As an example; a wheelbarrow-building book's out-of-sequence one-liners might be recorded in this order: Painting, Wheels, Assembly, Design, Packing, Safety, Engineering, Market Plans, Buying Materials, Model Variations, etc. All of which is hopelessly out of any useful or logical sequence for budding wheelbarrow builders. For sure, you would not tell them about assembly until after they designed and engineered the unit they plan to build.

Reviewing your TOC one-liners will indicate that most such chapter lines are in the wrong sequence. This is easy to fix. Number the lines in a more acceptable sequence and copy them in the renumbered order. Review this revision and consider it to be the flow of information in your book. Is the revised sequence more logical? If so leave it alone. You're lucky! Most of us do this revision thing a half dozen times before moving on. Should the chapter-line sequence please you not; change it again, and again, and again, until you're totally satisfied that this is the best possible order in which to present information to the buyer/reader. With such re-organization completed, input/type this draft TOC for extensive future use.

As you can appreciate, it's easy to do the reorganizing at this point. More difficult after chapters are written because for every later change of sequence you will be forced to adjust bridges between chapters. Bridges? These are concluding lines at the end of a chapter that alert the reader about what's coming next. Bridges are also first lines of the following chapter which remind the reader of what he/she read last night. My best suggestion is to review your draft TOC very carefully for hints of supportive chapters you should add. Such as for a book of recipes; the supportive chapters could be on health hints, refrigeration times for food, pot and pan selection, best tools for the kitchen and so on. Encourage your imagination to make the proposed book more rich; perhaps by including local references and sites if your book is a regional interest title such as about the town's history.

(Ed. Note: In the process of writing *Self Publishing Made Easy* the TOC was changed seven times. These changes included four complete resequencings of draft text which was obviously in the wrong position after being written.)

At this point you have listed every single chapter idea you considered appropriate. Now we consider size of the book. Our next go-around is to plan for chapter size. Sounds difficult but is really easy. Consider that your draft TOC represents, as it does, 100 percent of the work. Arbitrarily assign a percentage of space needed to fully deliver a message presenting the subject matter of each chapter. For example: Chapter A could become 5%, B 7%, C 2%, etc. Add them up. If you're over 100% by a wide margin, go through and take a polite nibble from each chapter's percentage.

Working Table of Contents

On the other hand, because this is all planning, if you're close to the 100% mark leave well enough alone. There will be plenty of give and take later as you merge adjacent two- and three-percent chapters if the subject matter is related. On the other hand, a 40- or 50-percenter should be cut into into smaller logical selections which will require additional TOC listings for the reduced-size chapters. Log the final acceptable percentage figure next to each chapter heading in the TOC for your permanent record. As to the total number of chapters, five are too few for the usual book. Ten to 15 is somewhat right and more if you are doing an all-out reference volume of depth or complexity.

At this same time write in a few additional information lines under each chapter title to remind you in supporting detail what you're going to write about. Besides, if you use these information lines in the book they can be fine-tuned to give potential book buyers more reasons to spend money. What you write in the TOC, and how well, not only jump starts the authoring process but could have a most favorable impact on sales of your book to smart buyers who may inspect the TOC first.

Final action in this time-consuming process is to use your chapter percentages to provide an idea of how many printed book pages should be allocated for each chapter. This is important because we're soon going to determine how much writing you should be prepared to do. Suppose the average competitive book has exactly 200-pages. Deduct ten pages for front and back matter

Working Table of Contents

(I'll detail this stuff later.) which leaves 190 remaining pages for text. Use the percentage figures you logged onto the TOC to determine how many pages you will allocate for each chapter. The 10% chapter amid those 190 pages has 19 book pages. The 4% chapter is more or less seven pages, and so on. Your sigh of relief is well justified. Now you've made a productive use for all the worry about the number of book pages and suchlike matters that we fussed with earlier while reviewing the competition. And you also have a thoughtfully estimated target as to the number of pages for each chapter of your proposed book. In the doing you are controlling ultimate publishing cost which is also spelled "profitability." This approach should be compared to writing without direction. That's when you might publish a fine book much too small to market, or too fat and expensive to merge, within the price range of comparable publications.

I hope the message is clear. More profit is made during preliminary planning than anywhere else in the building stage; be it books, bungalows or bridges.

As a side note, to make the world appear more friendly, log your book's working title across the top of the TOC page in bold type and sit back. This is what your published book could present to the potential buyer and reader.

Another detail in this area, and I admit there are even more details further on, is to compare what is accomplished to books reviewed during research.

Working Table of Contents

If your chapter and page count is close to the competition, leave well enough alone. More chapters is not all bad and impulse shoppers will consider the book of higher value. Fewer chapters in your book could be increased in number by splitting topics until your Table of Contents is at least average as compared to the competition.

There's no question but what page count is vital. Should you have created the TOC of a 100-page book, for a 200-page market, now's the time to adjust upward and at least become equal to the competition. On the other hand, should your planning have birthed a 350-page monster for that 200-page market, you could be increasing your cost of production to the point of losing money if priced near the average retail price for competitive books. Sure, by retaining the larger package size you are definitely more impressive, but real questions remain: Is your message worth the higher price you'll have to charge to show a reasonable profit and will your niche market buy books at that above-competition price?

Simple said. Low priced items sell in quantity. High priced items move in limited numbers or won't sell at all. Take your pick while designing your book.

Time is on your side. Invest all that is needed to continue adjusting your TOC up or down to make the book larger or smaller. These adjustments have cost you nothing. They do shift the odds in your favor when you actually begin to plan the writing of your book, in the following chapter.

Working Table of Contents

Your book project, such as we're organizing, is an important and costly venture. It would be a shame to face failure or economic loss because it did not fit the market on which it could sell best.

Revise nothing more and move on if you're comfortable. So far we've come up with a thoughtful estimate of the percentage of book pages for each chapter. In our next chapter we'll convert these percentages into an attainable target for your writing to come, which is best described as the number of words to write for each chapter.

Words Per Chapter

By taking time to write the "Synopsis" you distilled the essence of what you wanted to say. With "Marry the Market" you locked in the range coordinates of your buyer target. In the "Table of Contents" you organized the best-proportioned sequence of space allocation for presenting the message. Now is the right time to maintain the desired, and more importantly, profitable size of your book. But please keep in mind that while I continue to refer to "size of the book" what you are really going to do here and now, in this pre-production phase, is actually establish the length of the written manuscript and that is the number of words. Not number of book pages to which we'll return later when that area of adjustment becomes critical.

Words Per Chapter

The best support for the early determination of a percentage of chapter space, as I recommended in the preceding chapter, is that "Adequate is Enough." These are the words of Adam Osbourne, the genius who gave us our first useful portable computer/monitor with a carrying handle. And well do Adam's words apply to a profitable book. Reason enough to be comfortable using those arbitrary percentages of space per chapter that we established previously. At this point we're continuing to refine square footage (words) of the house (book), number and size of bedrooms, baths, pools, garages, etc. (separate chapters). So have fun as you will by estimating how many words each chapter of the proposed book should have because very soon you're going to enter the work area.

Writing to fit is important in the book trade where size/cost of the book, content and retail price, affects the amount of money to be made. On the other hand size is not a major factor in a mail-order project where advertisements sell the book and buyers seldom return a package no matter how bad it is. Fiction comes in the 85,000 word and up area but that's seldom a profitable area for self-publishing. Non-fiction is whatever you want to write and/or what matches the competition. My cautious suggestion for your proposed book is to write fully and gently overfill space allocated instead of coming up short. It's much easier to eliminate text than it is to fill space with words you didn't want to write in the first place.

Words Per Chapter

You, the writer/publisher, now have such a complete image of what's going into the book that estimated percentages of space required for each chapter will be remarkably accurate. You'll be more than pleased to find that the actual number of words you comfortably write for each section of the book will be a near match for those estimates.

In short, write completely because you can always delete text after you have done your best to present a worthwhile message of valid information for every reader.

What about art, photographs or charts? Are you planning to use them and if so, how many? Big is better because, when there's a shortage of words, art fills space. Tiny photos or indistinct charts are a turn off for anyone scanning random pages while considering purchase of a book. In my chapter "Write To Fit" I'll outline a simple method of inserting art or photographs should you be considering their use.

Now for the nitty gritty. One of the factors which determines how much writing you will do is the size of type on the finished book page. Work your way through the following for another area of decisions to be made while planning.

A few chapters back you were reviewing shelved competitive books and deciding on the physical size of your book and number of pages. Another item I firmly suggested you record was the size of type used in those books as indicative of the type you should specify. As an example: Consider that you are planning to use an

Words Per Chapter

8 pt. type in your book, which font may count to an average of 250 words on each book page. After creating the TOC, and considering your market, you estimated the percentage of pages each chapter should have. Accordingly the 19-page chapter is set for ten percent of the book. With 250 words per page times 19, your writing target is 4750 words for that specific chapter. Should you select a 10 pt. type, which may give you 200 words per page, you would need only 3800 words to fill the same 19-page chapter. Reason enough to now decide on the size type you plan to use, while recognizing that you may easily change it. Much later, when you edit and format the written material you have generated, you could enlarge the type size to make a gross shortage of words fill the book. Or reduce type size of the book's text to make room for additional material. Later, in "Computer Settings," I'll detail these techniques and such things as adjusting margins and number of lines per page, up or down, to modify the amount of space available on each page. When these techniques fail to meet your needs you can change the number of pages planned for the book which affects the size of your printing bill. For the time being, just keep it simple by selecting a competitive type size that you like.

To help you, the following lines provide comparison samples of the four type sizes used in this book.

Words Per Chapter

This is 11-point Schoolbook.

This is 11-point Italic Schoolbook.

This is 12-Point Bold Schoolbook.

This is 14-point Bold Schoolbook.

Based on your final selection of desired type size from a competitive book, do the word-count math for each chapter's percentage of pages estimate and note the resulting target number of words on the TOC for writing guidance. Later, as you write, enter the actual word count for each chapter next to the target word count on the TOC. This provides an easy way of controlling the size of your book. As you precede with writing and find that chapter word count is running long, write tightly. If you're consistently short of words per chapter begin to loosen up and write a bit on the long side.

Tell the story to the very best of your ability by using all the space available and be rewarded in finding that you are better than you thought. At this stage of self-publishing you've done so much brainstorming and planning, writing will flow easily and you'll be pleasantly expansive.

This book's early pages were drafted with a ball-point pen onto a steno pad while I enjoyed a shaded bank of the Mississippi river near a parkside coffee house. The draft was completed during a later vacation in California's Napa Valley wine country. As a result word count was totally unknown until all the hand-written text was stuffed into a compubeast.

If you are using a typewriter, and many of us often do in early stages of book development, word and page count is easy. A simple way to obtain the number of typed words is to count the words of ten full lines and move the decimal point one space left for number of words per line. A sample: Ten lines totaling 84 words is 8.4 words per line. Now count the number of lines per typewritten page. A sample: 29 Lines to each typewritten page or 8.4 times 29 comes up with 244 words per average page. If the typewritten manuscript totals ten pages you have 2440 words in that chapter. Adjust the number of typewritten pages you write, up or down, to provide the approximate number of words you need to fill or slightly overfill the book's chapters.

Easy to do with pencil and paper. Or ten fingers.

Computer users absolutely must spend a few dollars (Less than $100) for a publishing program. There's no need to buy a bloated marvel with every bell and whistle in the nerd world. Find something that will do word processing, provide maximum spell checking, offer a few reasonably useful fonts and print it all through a laser printer with header, footer and page numbers precisely in the manner you want for both manuscript editing and in your desired book format. In addition many computer publishing programs will count words which is super handy. You can use this same program to print paper hard-copies or "print to disk" for the book manufacturer who is going to produce your book from the computer disk..

It's fairly important that each chapter be a separate file on both the hard drive (for rapid access) and on a backup floppy in case the hard drive crashes. Give each chapter file a name that is specific, such as; My-Aunt.1 which will remind you that Chapter 1 is about your aunt. My-Uncle.2 is Chapter 2 about your uncle. Later it's easy to queue or merge these separate files into one long file. Before you make the final printout use the publishing program's Table of Contents and Index utilities to automatically produce those sections.

With "Adequate is Enough" our manta, the obligation is to make a reader capable while recognizing there's no way you can make him or her proficient. All you need do is closely review a few computer instruction books to realize how many technical writers totally cheat their readers by failing to communicate or meet this basic obligation of a good book. With all the preceding sermonizing and planning behind us, it's now time to write. This time, because you'll find it much easier than ever, let's embrace action in the next chapter.

Writing To Fit

This is the work area. You're home free to begin writing, or completing, the book.

The sigh of relief is well justified. Now you've reached productive use for all the worry about words, number of manuscript pages, and suchlikes we established earlier. You also enjoy a well designed editorial target in the TOC with its considered sequence of topics and text for your proposed book. Most importantly, by proceeding in this manner you have begun to control the cost and profitability of your project. I hope the message is clear. More profit is made during preliminary planning that anywhere else in the building of books, houses or Mississippi bridges; a point I've emphasized previously in hopes you will take it seriously.

Writing To Fit

How better to begin than with a clear idea of what you want to write and how you will design the resulting book to sell well in its potential marketplace?

In my work, by writing chapters in the sequence of a TOC, such as we organized a few chapters back, I manage to come up with a more cohesive book. In the early writing phase it may be best to write everything that you can think of even though we have established a target number of words. If you overwrite at this point, it is a blessing and no cause for alarm. Should a 6300 word chapter ends up with 10,000 words you may find the text so good that other chapters will be cut back or the book made larger.

If feels good, write it whichever way works. Why?

Because as you travel along this very special journey you'll have a mass of momentum in your favor and additional good ideas will surface to be incorporated into your writing. Let it happen. Insert text material out of sequence when it pops into your head. Worry not about where inserts are located for they can and will be moved later. I place such inserts apart with blank separation lines before and after the inserted block. Add topic suggestion notes in capital letters and you won't miss them. Just enjoy the pleasure of writing. Bogging down at this point, by revising text, editing or spell checking for nits and nats, derails the train of thought and causes it to become haphazard in creating a work that flows smoothly and is pleasant to read.

Writing To Fit

Once said; there are unlimited other ways to write a book. Many authors polish each chapter as it is completed then move on to writing the next. Some do the last chapter first, and a successful few write snippets over a random period time and cello-tape them into a book. Hopefully this latter group also writes enough bridges to merge their snippets together. I prefer to write fully, then review all my research for additional material to be added into free-flowing chapters I've become fully familiar with. Text blocks or inserts from one area of the book can be moved to their more appropriate position during editing and sequence revision sessions. Side notes, such as the following are acted upon while editing text.

NEED BRIDGE

Pictures, charts and suchlike are a headache; even to professional layout artists. Here's the way I do it; which works well and is not too complicated. I evaluate each piece of art and write on a stickie, or the art's backside, my opinion of how much space, in vertical inches, it will occupy. Suppose I have a page-wide picture that appears to require four inches of open space (a window) as measured from top to bottom. There will be a caption below the picture so I add additional room (such as a half-inch) for caption text. As I write original text, or while editing, and reach the place in the manuscript where that piece of art is to be inserted, I type a single line all in capitals.

ART 9-A 4-1/2 INCHES.

Writing To Fit

This note will be acted on, and 4-1/2 inches of space made available for Picture 9-A, when I'm formatting the final pages as described a few chapters later in "Computer Settings" and "Proofing To Print."

Because actually writing (or completing) your book is a do-it-now project, I'm going to switch this discussion to a most important area. That is the time, not the craft, of writing a book. My from-experience recommendations are those procedures which work well for me. I write for a reasonable period of time, such as four to six hours, about five days each week. For the book you are reading, short breaks within the four or five days kept the brain from frying under my modest conceptual stress and encouraged free thinks to flow easily. As I mentioned earlier, the initial draft of *Self Publishing Made Easy* was hand-written while I was happily relaxed by a gazebo on Wisconsin banks of the Mississippi River. The final portion of the draft was not completed until six months later during additional vacation time in California's Napa Valley. The hand-written draft was logged onto a computer disk in the most simple manuscript format you can imagine. Justification was turned off to eliminate the editing bother of automatic hyphenation. After stuffing the computer with this very rough unedited text I tallied a word and line count of each chapter and recorded this information at the bottom of the final page. It was printed at 25 lines per page with wide margins on the left, so there would be room for notes, and double line spacing for inserting additional text.

Writing To Fit

Chapter name and number were in the header with manuscript page number and date in the bottom footer. The result was, in effect, my first opportunity to read this book which has passed a dozen rewritings.

Which brings us to a question. What should you write with? If you prefer typewriting install a brand new ribbon to keep from displaying popped eyeballs while reading and re-reading massive amounts of dim typing. It's easy to double-line space and set wide margins both left and right. After the manuscript is complete a computer service operator can re-key your material, or scan the typewriting onto a disk without the trouble of keyboarding. Scanning also makes the fresh ribbon important to meet needs of the Optical Character Recognition (OCR) program which scoops typing off the page and translates it into computereze. After scanning, all you need do is run a spell check of each file to correct odd words the character reading program messed. The resulting files can be printed out for editing on hard copy. Print on paper is much better to edit because it more closely relates to what the book buyer will see. Besides, when editing it is far easier to shuffle sheets of paper as compared to clicking through a shimmering monitor screen while jumping from one disk file to another.

A publishing program's manuscript page format, with its double-line spacing and the wide margins, provides plenty of space for editing notes and correction on the printed drafts. A second reminder: Be certain that you set the computer program so that the footer of every printed page carries the date, file identification and page number somewhat as the following, C:\Pubbook\Pubfront.BOD Pg 81 3/14/99, for this chapter. All you need do is drop a handful of manuscript sheets on the floor, then try to sort them out, to make you a true believer in the full worth of individual page identification. By setting this information into Header and Footer add-ons of the program it prints automatically on every page.

My most valuable writing-to-fit instruction is to back up each day's work onto a separate floppy so you archive at least two complete copies of your efforts. You'll never forgive yourself if a "crash" takes place and you face beginning all over again. 'Nuf said.

Let's reconsider what should be in computer programs. To begin with, a simple "word-processing program" can be made to do part of the book production job. But it's such a hassle that I recommend you forget it. A "publishing program," for less than $100, will usually have the following features: The ability to print common type sizes such as 8 pt., 10 pt., 12 pt., etc. With useful fonts such as Times Roman, Schoolbook or similar easy-reading faces such as those used in newspapers and books. Many programs have a means of printing sample pages of every type face they offer. Run the samples in common point sizes and make your selection of a fairly large (10, 11 or 12 pt.) type for your manuscript with larger being better. You'll use a bit more paper for printouts but large type makes the frequent manuscript readings, editings and revisions that much easier. Note that now we're only speaking about size of type for manuscript pages, not the type size used in book-text page calculations mentioned in the chapter on competition.

A spell checker is priceless as long as you keep in mind that both "hill" and "mill" are spelled correctly. Your fingers may have hit the wrong key and you're not inputting what you really intended to write.

It's fairly important that whichever publishing program you buy offers the ability to print out in the Postscript format. This is necessary because, as this book is being published, CTP (Computer To Press) is coming into extensive use in the book printing business. With this system you merely send your selected printer one or more disks bearing your book in a Postscript format he will specify; plus a hard-copy print-out made in your office. He will run your disks on his equipment, verify that he is processing your book as you wish, then output the disk directly to his printing press and print your book. This eliminates a number of steps such as photographing the hard copy, taping the resulting film onto a set of paper masks then exposing the film to a large printing plate. CTP is a much faster production method and will eventually bring about a reduction in book costs. I'll cover this in great detail in the later chapter, "The Best Printing Price," when you'll be ready to consider its use while negotiating with book manufacturers.

In this computer literate world it may appear to be redundant to point out that all computers were not created equal. Buying one by mail seems to work best if from the original manufacturer and you are assured of receiving the latest model before placing an order. But no matter where you purchase, insist that every program be installed and working in perfect order. With the hardware must be installation discs for all programs and complete manuals for your frustration. Then plan to set aside enough time for a dedicated learning period to get the new beast to heel on command. Warranties and service vary all over the block and such assets are spelled out in the fine print. Best is on-site service where your unit is cared for in your office. Not only do you enjoy service on need but you have a live person to question about the mysteries of operation. I've had pleasant warranty service such as when a new HP unit went down a few days after receipt. Hewlett-Packard had a replacement at my door within 24 hours. On the other hand, a local vendor replaced a computer's fan, at no charge, while I waited. Good service in one instance from a well-known major manufacturer and in the other situation from a small chain of local stores that had been in business for years.

If you're serious about being profitable your book must be written within a reasonable time frame. Which underscores all my previous emphasis on planning and organizing the pre-production of your publishing project before writing begins or you complete the manuscript on hand.

Writing To Fit

The guidelines in *Self-Publishing Made Easy* have been refined from nearly 50 productive publishing years and enough resulting successes to assure me they are useful. Different methods of book design exist but until you find or develop them read on and shift the odds of profitable publishing in your favor.

Now it's your turn. Write a complete book without editing, revising or re-organizing. After you're finished, print that initial computer or typewritten draft, kick back and enjoy the exquisite pleasure of the first reading of your words on paper. At long last, your book is born. Squalling, red-faced from mispellings, not really very attractive but it's all yours to nurture into a full-fledged success; with a first reading the next thing to be done.   (Yes, it is misspellings !)

The First Reading

With the entire book now printed in manuscript form, you can give it a fast reading while ignoring glitches to be fixed later. Your draft is the wonderful result of writing, writing, and writing everything one can think of that could possible be important to the buyer and reader of your book. Be not critical. Polish nothing. Please; no spell check, no punctuation fixed and worsened syntax be damned. However, did you make a set of backup files of every chapter? Did your format program automatically insert the file identification code and date on each printed page? If these technical bits are under control move on and casually review each chapter for a "feeling" as to paragraphs reading in the best sequence. If they're not you may consider resequencing as necessary.

The First Reading

Should you elect to re-sequence, an easy chapter reorganization method is to code each paragraph with a letter of the alphabet: A, B, C etc. Log these codes on a separate sheet of paper with a one-line description of paragraph contents beside its code letter. Re-sequence the one-liners into a new numeric order so paragraph topics flow from one to the other in improved order. Finally, go back to the original material to shift manuscript paragraphs into the new numeric order. It's easy to use the alphabet code to find its appropriate paragraph and "block move" or "cut" the paragraph a revised numeric sequence with an "insert" or "paste" at its new location. If your material is typewritten, scissor paragraphs apart and cello tape them in the improved sequence.

Now; another fast read and continue to ignore glitches.

Paragraph sequencing should be much better. If you find paragraphs that continue to seem out of place, they can be moved again to an improved location as easily as you moved them the first time.

Print out or retype the resequenced material and enjoy. Though there's much work ahead, this is the highly satisfying business of polishing a brand new and most worthwhile product.

Training your book to be socially (profitably) successful is the next pleasure. Be not too critical of the second draft's printout. It's rough and valuable exactly as it is. Give it another fast read by ignoring spelling, syntax and other such embarrassments to provide a valuable impression of what you have. You're enjoying an overview of the Grand Canyon, not the pebbles and boulders of creation. If it feels good, it is good. If you're not comfortable that's an okay to dig in and continue the fixes which follow herein.

After reviewing the resequenced chapter text, and your happy heart slows a bit, go back and read the entire book all over again. This time we're only interested in chapter sequence, not paragraph sequence. Do chapters appear to be in the desired (best) order? If not, renumber and/or rename them again. How about chapter content? Does text fit the chapter title? No problem. If content and title conflict, rename the chapter and/or move it elsewhere to improve things. Again determine if the text you moved inside each chapter flows in more logical sequence from opening lines to ending transfer or bridge to the next chapter. If so, leave it alone. If not, use that infamous red pen (It should be red for changes to be easily found.) to mark text for relocation. Then scribble in text bridges which carry the reader smoothly from a preceding chapter into the following chapter.

This bridge thing is fairly important. As you end a chapter there should be enough text to advise the reader about what is coming up in the next chapter and how it supports what they have completed reading. As the following chapter begins its text insert a few words which continue or enhance the flow of thought from the preceding chapter. I've tried to do this all through *Self Publishing Made Easy*. You may

The First Reading

find it helpful to review my chapter to chapter bridges and look for jumps I missed or those I should have written in a more acceptable fashion.

Please keep in mind that these early readings are all about "quick and dirty" inserting, editing and changing based on feelings rather than logic. We'll do the nit-picking later. So swing away and enjoy such stress-less improving to the best of your ability. After these early revision chores are accomplished turn back to your files and revise the TOC to reflect the newly modified sequence of chapters in your book; that is if you made any adjustments. A spell check becomes useful at this point to pick up irritating errors and make subsequent editing more peaceful. Lastly run another word and line count of each chapter to be logged at the bottom of the last page of the chapter to keep track of what you are doing. This effort provides three data; pages, lines and words to compare with target estimates you noted on the draft TOC that was created during planning of the book.

Now print the book out again in manuscript form, as a third draft, for some really serious basic editing. Perchance you've not outguessed me, I'm again recommending that you always read and edit printed paper pages of your manuscript. A single exception to this recommendation surfaces later.

This third manuscript draft will be great fun. Your book baby is beginning to talk back. You can enjoy it and polish to your heart's content. It will reward you with great pleasure. Chapters are now in

The First Reading

their best sequence and paragraphs are coupling smoothly because you have stroked them with small bits of spit and polish. Hopefully you now agree with me that it was far easier to flip back and forth through sheets of paper, while seeking the proper place for homeless good stuff. This method compares to endless scrounging through a number of computer files on the disk and messing with lines of text glaring at you from the computer's monitor screen.

The entire text is yours for critical content review and adjustment of word choice, syntax, spelling and punctuation. Worry not about what you writing because you are the expert in that area. I am only (and that "only" is significant) seriously concerned with how you are writing. Mark corrections on sheets of the draft printout using the red pen while fussing over every single thing that strikes a discordant note. For sure, this printout will be a mess of notes and corrections. The more the merrier will make your published results that much better.

Keyboard these corrections into your computer files. Run another spell check and print out a fourth manuscript draft. This one makes for more good vibes because you can continue to read for pleasure. Enjoy what you doing at the same time you appreciate the useful sequence of chapters, paragraphing and flow of text from chapter to chapter. Look closely for areas of information you failed to disclose to your satisfaction. And how about the page and word count? Should your manuscript be undernourished, decisions are needed.

The First Reading

Consider writing more text for those chapters which are a bit lean, or consider marketplace factors affecting a decision to reprice or resize the book into a less expensive market. On the other hand if your book is becoming too big to be profitable on the intended market there is a need to revise your price objectives or consider the most painful step of all; eliminating priceless prose to make the book smaller. Alternatives are modifying the type size, or changing margins and number of lines per page; all of which are less painful than deleting text. I'll get into technical adjustments a bit later because for now I only want to worry you a bit about what's ahead.

All of which underscores the real purpose of the book you are reading: *Self Publishing Made Easy*. It is imperative that you create a profitable package. Few booksellers will have interest in a book that is too expensive for its field, or one with contents so underwhelming they do not justify any price.

The "blood sweat and tears" of writing justifies biting the bullet to firm your commitment to creating a compliment to your bank account and fan club.

Anyhow, there's enough guidance in this and preceding chapters to revise and adjust to your heart's content. After chapter files are updated, corrected and/or re-sequenced, read each one on the computer screen. This sudden shift, away from reading paper manuscript printouts, is valuable as a nit picker. You will find the monitor to be such a totally different presentation of text that your eye will find glitches you

The First Reading

failed to notice on paper. Take our word for it, a statement cynics usually view as an invitation to trouble and eventual begin-all-over-again blues.

In sum, early editing is an imprecise art and every method has virtues and vices you can use to your advantage. Such as switching horses (paper to monitor) in mid-stream to determine what else is new or needs fixing. However, this is not the time to relax. I assure you there is more to fix after we move on to "Copy Flow and Text Editing" in the next chapter. These two areas are your true objectives in all this formatting business wherein we seek to give the book buyer an easy read with the multiple satisfactions of useful communication.

Copy Flow And Text Editing

Find your senior editor's hat and pop it on.

Here's where you will be encouraged to become really tough and nit-pick the dickens out of your work while making it better and better in the process. What's to be done now is carefully read the manuscript twice, each reading with a totally separate attitude. The first go-through (Copy Flow) is only concerned with how words flow from beginning to end. The second attitude (Text Editing) is to fine-tune punctuation and text to be as coherent as you can make them.

Sure, you have already completed paragraph and chapter sequencing and early draft editing but they were simply reorganizing the obvious. Here you dig down to the tiniest nits of the nitty-gritty and make sure every single sentence and thought is in the desired sequence while leading or flowing smoothly into the next thought. To be painfully obvious; what you are doing is to make sure your text fits the readability parameters of "One thought, one sentence. One action, one paragraph. One topic, one chapter." Okay?

So let's talk about doing a Copy Flow edit.

Copy flow begins with again determining if you need any additional final-lines of text added to a preceding paragraph to make it flow easily into the following paragraph. And, obviously, does that following paragraph need any early text modified to smooth the flow of information from the preceding paragraph. It's abrupt changes of thought, from one paragraph to another, or one chapter to another, that are destructive to communication. Again, sequence, sequence and sequence. Is everything in the best order for easy learning or must the reader churn back and forth in a paragraph, or through a chapter, to figure out what it is you are explaining. You'll recognize this as the bridges you were concerned with in the previous chapter of *Self Publishing Made Easy*. Here you review them all again to make your book better than ever.

How about the same question as related to subject matter making a smooth transition from chapter to chapter? Does text carry your subject smoothly from Chapter 3 to the opening words of Chapter 4, or whichever? Are you telling them how to build the wheelbarrow before you suggest they buy the materials? Or presenting some similar jump in illogic? Of course, early in this book I had you organizing chapters for logical sequence. But in the continual rewriting, paragraph shifting and rethinking that's taken place it is reasonably possible you could have changed the emphasis of a complete chapter. Or it may have been moved elsewhere to establish a more reasonable sequence of information. Such moves demand our present need for additional attention to modified bridges and copy flow inside the separate chapters of your book.

Do any chapters seem too short to be useful? This is a good time to attach them to a preceding, or following chapter and smooth the text merge. What about chapters that still continue to go on forever? Consider cutting them into even smaller sections or merging with others before or behind to reorganize an entire area into more readable text. Easy to do now. More difficult to do later after you have your book formatted with the TOC and Index completed and ready for the printing press.

There's more to look for in Copy Flow editing. Short sentences are better than long. Long sentences are useful because variation in sentence length, like tone changes of music, makes for emphasis. Short is action. Long is scenery or description. Yes, I said this was not a book about writing. However I ask you to look upon the above as not intruding on your skills but as friendly reminders. But, enough of Copy Flow.

Copy Flow And Text Editing

Your next go through is Text Editing.

A heavy-handed red pen is the help-mate here as you zoom in on information glitches and whip your package into greater perfection. Hit the syntax bit hard to make sure your selection of words, and the tense of sentences and paragraphs, really comes off the way you intended to impress the searching reader. Does punctuation help or get in the way? Be good to yourself by spreading this very difficult phase of editing over a period of time. Otherwise you may become bored, irritated or tired, and gloss over terribles that no self-respecting writer would be happy to see in print. Worst of all with said writer's name prominently displayed on the cover.

Spell check the hard way, with eyeballs, while giving the text a careful read and looking for such upsets as the computer checker approving "mall" for "maul," "you" for "your" or similars. While you're at it, in addition to seeking unusual spelling errors, seek those not-so-obvious punctuation deletions or text clarifications in need of adjustment.

These two separate edits are the most rewarding polishing phases of publishing a profitable book. On completion you are more than entitled to lean back with a glow of pride. Your book will be in sharp focus as a valuable contribution to its readers. Best of all, the work you've been doing is downslope from here. Upgrading text is relatively satisfying and with every draft you will become more and more encouraged at the nearing of successful publication.

Copy Flow And Text Editing

I hope you didn't ignore my point that that two separate editings were involved here. The first reading was for sequential flow. The second was for punctuation, spelling, syntax and other mishaps. This separation of inspections is very important from my point of view. I always do a better job editing for only one thing at a time. Perhaps you can do both at once and make me feel badly. Either way; what works is right.

The methodology of spit and polish comes up in the following chapter where I'll justify importance and usefulness of multiple draft-manuscript printouts as you continue preparing your completed book for the printing press.

Drafts, Drafts, Drafts

If you believe I should justify the great number of revisions and draft printouts that I recommend, here's the justification.

The cost of desk-top laser-printing a book's draft manuscript is slightly more or less than $10. Should you print ten drafts of the manuscript you're investing about $100 to insure publishing a better than average book. Those few dollars are well spent to assure a quality product and tilt the odds in your favor of profiting from the considerable time and the many thousands of dollars in a self-publishing project.

I recommend drafts, and many of them, as critical to success.

It's your choice.

And your money.

Computer Settings

It's super-easy to detour around this chapter if you're not using a computer. This material is not for you. If authoring by hand, or with a typewriter, after the book manuscript is finaled with all the recommended adjustments, take your work to a computer service bureau. Have them input the text onto a disk for laser printing in a book format that you specify for reproduction by the book manufacturer. However this excursion to an outside vendor may involve enough money that you could buy a used computer and do inputting and the laser-printing at home.

Be that as it may. Computer-based "publishing programs" are so common that I'm proceeding on the basis that you are going to buy or are now using one.

Computer Settings

Whichever; good publishing programs are able to format your laser printouts so the sheets present the exact appearance of your book pages. Type size, font and number of lines per page will print as you have designed the desired finished product.

On the assumption that you are computer-based, let's move on. With the many current changes taking place among book manufacturing concerns it's important that the publishing program you have, or are purchasing, will output text files to a disk in the Postscript (PS) or Portable Document File (PDF) format. Both of these are in common use by book production printers. In these formats you "print" the book to a floppy disk or storage media in the same manner as sending it to your desktop printer. From this disk the distant book production house can translate bytes and bits of text directly to a printing plate or negative. This eliminates the costly steps of photographing your paper printout (hard copy), making a negative, then imaging the negative onto the printing plate. Accordingly, there are some cost savings to you in the CTP (Computer to Press) and DTP (Direct to Plate) procedures. Another important advantage is in the improved quality of reproduction of art in your book because they (CTP/DTP) eliminate two steps, photographing your art and making negatives, from the prepress operation. Bluelines, which are preliminary paper prints of the book, are not common for proofing work in either of these two procedures. Instead the printer can send you a proof

Computer Settings

over the telephone line for viewing on your monitor, or by outputting their CTP or DTP disks to a laser printer in their shop send you hard-copy pages to review. An advantage of this latter procedure is that such digital proofs can be made in black and white or in full color on the very same paper your book and cover will be printed on. A disadvantage is that no longer can the printer make corrections or additions. Changes can only be processed by the printer from new disks you produce in your office. Offsetting advantages are that to make changes, all you need do is modify the computer disk at your desk and send the new disk off to the book manufacturer. In addition your entire book could be archived by the printer on a digital tape or disk backup. Need more books? All the printer does is output your book's computer disk and begin printing much sooner than if you had to mail them a set of hard-copy pages or return original negatives from the first printing.

The benefits of sending only disks to the printer increase in proportion to the volume and size of the work. As an example: In 1998 The Book of the Month Club was producing 18 catalogs a year. Their digital cameras and scanners feed into, and select from, more than 10,000 image files to produce 2000 catalog pages a year. Seven people do it all. And TBOMC saves $1.5 million annually with CTP.

Look through the Index of the publishing program's User Manual for an instruction entry usually listed as "Page Layout/Setup" or

Computer Settings

"Format/Formatting." No matter how the manual lists it, you should be able to find something about book formats with instructions on how to make simple adjustments to the program. With that bit of background behind us, return to the competitive sample books you purchased during your market research ("Competition"). Select the size book you want to produce, such as 5-1/2 by 8-1/2, 6 by 9, or 8-1/2 by 11 inches. Measure top, bottom and side margins of your best-liked book and duplicate them with your publishing program settings. There's nothing complicated here. The computer program will do everything automatically after you feed in the appropriate information. This saves you tons of money as compared to having the book printer do the job. When setting computer format margins for a book please remember that inside margins, known as "gutters" in the book trade, are wider than outside left and right margins to allow for the binding process. Should this be a bit confusing; measure the top, bottom, outside and gutter margins of *Self-Publishing Made Easy* for both left and right pages. Headers are at the top of the page, footers at the bottom. They are lines of text or page numbers which repeat from page to page throughout the book. By following the publishing program's instructions you can set a header which is usually the name of the chapter, and a footer, such as used for this book which reads *"Self Publishing Made Easy."* Page numbers will be correctly sequenced at the top or bottom of each page. Also look for "Widow" and "Orphan" control settings which I recommend you use. They will be explained in detail later on but, for the time being, just toggle them active to make your life easier. Select the book's type style (font) you like best and the size of that font (8-, 10-, 12-point). This is the same decision area you worked with while setting up your manuscript format. This time the decision is more a matter of matching the competition's books. A new one to work with is the distance between the lines known as 4 lpi, 6 lpi, 7 lpi, etc. This translates to four lines per inch, six lines per inch and so on. Following are samples of line spacing to clarify my comments. After you inspect them, plan ahead to run off a sample chapter of your book with three or four different line spacings. You can select the easiest to read and most visually pleasing. It's a worthwhile experience to observe the changes in readability and book page appearance resulting from such modest adjustments as those following. Text line spacing for this book is 4.50 lines per inch.

This line and the following are set at 4 lpi.

This line and the following are set at 4 lpi.

This line is 4 lpi from those above.

This line and the following are set at 6 lpi.
This line and the following are set at 6 lpi.
This line is 6 lpi from those above.

This line and the following are set at 7 lpi.
This line and the following are set at 7 lpi.
This line is 7 lpi from those above.

Self Publishing Made Easy

Computer Settings

After your publishing program has been adjusted to produce a book-page layout comparable to your best-liked competition, copy four or five pages of your manuscript text into a page-layout test file (A:\Test.Bk) on a fresh disk and print it out as though it were for the book. Using the test file as a practice pad, approve or adjust everything from margins to type, to headers/footers and line count per page. To open up space for art in the text use the Enter key to add empty lines to give each piece of art the required number of inches where it relates to the text. Four inches for a photo, with text set at 6 lpi, calls for 23 additional "Enters" plus three more for the half-inch three-line caption mentioned much earlier. When laser printed your book pages will reproduce with blank spaces (windows) for the art which I'll tell you how to fill later when that bit of action is necessary. For what it's worth, "art" as used herein is the generic description for drawings, graphs, photographs and whatever else of that genre you can think of which differs from plain text. Because your test pages are in the same format a bookstore shopper will inspect they merit close review. Are those sample pages what you really want? How do they compare to the competition? Is the type font and size what you believe will do best in the book? Remember, this is now a sample of book pages and not manuscript pages wherein we used large type just to make it easy reading. If the tested book-page format is okay, move on! If not, adjusting the book's final format all over again is free with only a

Computer Settings

few sample pages are involved. Once you have a printout that is satisfactory, record all the computer program's format settings and adjustment selections onto a reference card. This memorandum will be most useful should you find additional changes are needed later to modify page size or presentation.

Formatted page numbers printed in the upper left and right corners, or centered at the bottom of the page, are equally satisfactory. The name of the chapter may print left, right or centered at the top of each text page while your book's title usually prints centered at the bottom of the page. Smaller or slightly different type may be used for each of these page informations to set them off from the text or make them more easily useful for the searching reader.

Lastly, two things. The first line of the first paragraph of each chapter is not indented. Set that line to print flush left. And that same first paragraph of each chapter should begin a noticeable number of lines below top-margin location of text on following pages. Check competition and this book for other typical design treatments you may wish to adopt.

It's best to create brand new book files to completely reformat the manuscript material you've been working with. The reason is simple. If you mess up an original file all is lost. Mess up a duplicate and it's not a problem. Copy each finaled manuscript chapter into a separately-named disk file such as "A:\Chptr1.Bk" which translates to "Chapter One of Book" on the "A" floppy. You could do up to 999

Computer Settings

chapters with this code. Publishing programs, including the one I use, allow you to establish the basic book-page format and then hit a single key to reformat such copied manuscript material into that new form. Please, as I suggested a few lines back, only do reformatting on a copy of your manuscript's chapter file after you have made backup files of everything. Backup files are a dandy security blanket on the off chance you'd crash.

After the publishing program reformats that first chapter, have it count the words. Record the word, line and page count shown on the computer's monitor screen, below the last line of the chapter. Most publishing programs have a method of marking such notes as "Non Printing" so they will not print out on the finished book page but you can view the data anytime you need guidance.

Now that you have everything programmed and formatted, use the "A;\Chptr1.Bk" file to print out the first chapter of your book. Review it thoughtfully and do any additional rework including further adjustment of type size for text, location of headers, footers and page numbers until you achieve a page design that sparkles. This is creativity for which layout artists earn tons of money while slaving away in a large publishing house. They keep the money but have to please a boss. You do it for free while pleasing yourself and future buyers of your book. A neat tradeoff.

Now for a pair of clinkers.

Computer Settings

The simple method of solving every book's widow-orphan problem was mentioned early in use of your publishing program's widow/orphan control procedure. Nevertheless you may find a page with one or two lines of text at the top, which are final lines of a paragraph from the preceding page. You have found "widows." They're easy to make happy with a little TLC. Go to the preceding page and take out words or merge two paragraphs so the widows jump backward onto the previous page where they belong. You can watch this happen on the monitor screen. Or you can fatten widows by writing additional text for any preceding paragraphs which will force a few additional lines over into the former widow area. It's all a matter of appearance wherein three or more lines at the top of a page seems to appear satisfactory, one or two are a bit strange and plead for fixing.

On the other hand when you find a page with one or two beginning lines of a paragraph all alone at the bottom of the preceding page, with the rest of the paragraph on the following page, you have "orphans." The easy fix for this one is to insert blank lines above the orphans and kick them over to the following next page. The hard part of all this is that it must begin with page one and work to the end of each chapter because each change affects all following lines of that chapter. Somewhat of an "I told you so," here's where you'll really appreciate each chapter as a separate file. Orphans also occur at the end of a paragraph, such as "word."

Computer Settings

Unfortunately the final paragraph of each chapter is excluded from the widow/orphan control bit and you must fix them yourself. Otherwise chapters could end with a nearly blank page displaying only one or two lines of text at the top. The fix is easy. Write a lot of new text to fill the near-empty page or remove a bit of text from the preceding page to pull the widow forward to the preceding page.

It's a very good idea to use this same first chapter for a test workout of the publishing program's indexing procedure. Most publishing programs allow you to select a word for indexing, punch a key and the program automatically indexes the selected word with a link to the page number. You may be able to move that indexed word anywhere in the book and the index would always print out with the correct page number. The procedure is critical and because all publishing programs seem to do it differently, the best I can recommend is to follow the instruction manual. The caution here is to practice your skills and the program on those test chapter pages. Life will be much happier with small mistakes made while learning than from indexing the entire book incorrectly. After test indexing you should "Run" the index program. This will alphabetize all the words you have marked for indexing and place the correct page number next to the word in an "Index" listing file. The sequence is to now laser print your test chapter then separately print the one-chapter index listing. Each entry will point to the page bearing the indexed word. A real time-saver.

Computer Settings

Later, I'll explain indexing by hand with pad and pen which is the hard way and the last, last, thing done.

From here on you are working with book pages, which are a completely different set of marbles than the previous manuscript pages. The going gets a bit rough so read slowly. From printing out and adjusting that first (test) chapter you now know how your book will appear to the public. Use that confidence to adjust every following chapter file, one at a time, using the same procedure. By printing chapters in the desired book format you will soon know how many text pages your finished book is likely to contain. Suppose you are working toward a book of 200 pages as the desired package suggested by competitive titles. If you're in the ballpark leave the present 200 alone. On the other hand your total printout may contain too many text pages for your budget or market. If so, now's the time to experiment with one-chapter changes of type size and/or font. If you don't like your book's pages full of Times Roman, try Garamond or Century Schoolbook. And/or decide on a slightly condensed type, wherein the characters are closer together, which will place more words on each book page. Or drop from 10 pt. to 9 pt. size type which also increases the number of words to a page. You can modify the number of lines per inch by placing lines closer together such as changing from 6 lpi (Six lines per inch.) to 7 lpi. You could reduce the size of art, eliminate a few pictures, or increase the number of lines per page by narrowing top and bottom margins. Setting lines longer, by narrowing left and right margins, will give you more words per page. Adjust the test chapter to reflect your changes and print it out again for another inspection. Suppose your initial format selection placed an average of 250 words on each of those test pages from a 10-point font. This would be 2500 words for ten book pages Should you drop to 8-point type, and achieve a possible 20 percent increase in number of words per page, the new format of 300 words per page would require only a bit over eight book pages for 2500 words. This 20 percent reduction in page count will reduce your 200-page book to about 160 pages. It's your call. All of this current hassle is much less expensive than reviewing a completed book ready for production before you realize it's all wrong. With a simple caveat. For a book to be sold on the open market, size is important. Big is better. Small is cheaper. Adjust accordingly with an eye on the competition.

A contrary problem in page control is working with a format of 250 words on a page when you have only 30,000 words in the manuscript. 250 Into the 30,000 gives you a book of 120 pages. But research disclosed that most competitive books were offering 150-175 pages. Obviously your 120 page product is not going to be very impressive on the bookseller's shelf. The fix here is to enlarge the art, go to a larger type size, such as from 8-point, to 10- or 12-point, increase width of margins top, bottom and sides and expand line spacing from six lines per inch to five. With a lot of luck you could modify everything and end up with 200 words per book page. The 200 into 30,000 will give you a 150 page book which is at the lower end of the competition. You won't be the most impressive but at least you can hold your own with a sharp cover, more authentic text, additional references and a huge index. Following is a selection of two fonts displaying how the length of printed lines changes as style characteristics vary in width.

Observe the length of this line of type.

Observe the length of this line of type.

They're both the same 11-point size but one is in the Roman font and the other is in Italic. Different font styles, such as Schoolbook vs. Times Roman, will provide much longer or shorter line lengths to meet your needs. The section above sampled the appearance of only two faces (Roman and Italic) available from the many fonts in a publishing program. Of particular importance for your consideration is the space each font needs to present a common series of letters. Letters closer together give you more words per page. Those farther apart will reduce the number of words per page. Review the choices in your publishing program and enjoy the experience of design selection by printing out the sample chapter in a variety of presentations and modifications of type you like best.

If you have no photographs, art and charts, skip the next few paragraphs because we're going to use the windows established by the insertion of empty lines per inch. For example: 24 Empty lines in a six-lines-per-inch format is four inches of window space for your artwork. Should you have modified the lines per inch, say from six to five, or six to seven, you have reduced or increased white space for art. Fix the space for art right now or you'll hate yourself for outputting the newly revised book only to find that none of the art fits properly. In a subsequent chapter I'll review some of the practical methods for physically or computerly inserting art.

When you continue to face problems with page count, keep in mind that an Index could occupy more or less space by using these same techniques. Or you could set it in either one or two columns to gently solve a page-count difficulty.

This is an area of book designing you'll have to sort out. As your review of competition disclosed, there are no standards and the best I can do is give you reasonable options and techniques for your serious consideration. Besides, in the next chapter we get into the business of Front and Back Matter which messes with page count. 'Taint easy but its your money that's on the line, with time involved being the trading material. A few extra minutes or hours here could reduce the cost of your book and increase profits, or help price the book in a more competitive manner in search of increased sales.

Front And Back Matter

In the last chapter we organized your computer to print out a complete (almost, that is) book in the book-page format. But there were two important sections missing which I'll now add in measured doses to reduce confusion.

One section, which makes up early pages of the book, is known as "front matter." It is those pages which precede text of the book. Front matter can use as few as three, or more, pages if you wish. Some of this material is absolutely, positively, undeniably important. Other front matter is useful but, depending on space available and your personal preferences, may be omitted in favor of limiting page count.

Front And Back Matter

If you wish to number front matter pages use Roman numerals: I, II, III, etc. Right-hand pages are odd numbers, like I, III, V, etc. Left hand pages are even, like II, IV, VI , etc.

The first page (I), which faces the inside surface of the front cover, is usually blank and displays no page number. However it may carry the title of your book but no other information. In this instance it is described as bearing the "Bastard Title" for a devious reason that somehow escapes me.

The second page (II), on the back side of that first page (I), is blank. It's best used as a place for your autograph (No ! Never your checking account signature.) and the date of your author signing.

The third page (III) displays the title of your book with the author's name and that of the publishing house. You can fancy this page with art or run it plain vanilla depending on what's in competitive books and/or your approach to morality.

The fourth page (IV) is loaded. Here's where you repeat the title, author's name, printing sequence for the specific title, edition number, International Standard Book Number (ISBN), Library of Congress (LC) number, whatever else you want and, for sure, the Copyright Notice. You may wish to add the notation "All rights reserved" to place eager beavers on notice of ownership determination and animosity toward plagiarism or unauthorized reproduction.

Front And Back Matter

Page five (V) is for a dedication or author's comments about the book or his/her philosophy.

Six (VI) is usually blank, but don't ask me why.

The seventh page (VII), a right-hander, is the first or only page of the "Table of Contents" (TOC) which can be headed as simply "Contents." This one you complete after the rest of the book is finaled.

Now you're almost home free and can fill or not fill the following pages in this order: Preface, Foreword, list of Illustrations, list of Tables or Graphs, Acknowledgments of Assistance and the Introduction. These are all numbered in the Roman style and each should begin on a right hand page. Keep in mind that these latter goodies cost money because they're adding pages to your book. Other than the obligatory first title (Page III), page of required information (Page IV), and Contents you may omit and adjust front matter to suit yourself and in the doing be enough different that booksellers could consider your book not up to trade standards and decline to stock it. Consider asking a friendly authority to write a Foreword for your book. It'll be most impressive if there's a string of letters after the supportive authority's name, such as M.D., PhD, D.V.M. or suchlike. If one is good, more is better. Authorities could also be asked to write an Introduction, Preface, flap note and/or back cover recommendation. For examples see food store paperbacks which are often loaded with such selling messages to impress the casual browser.

Front And Back Matter

If front matter ends on a right hand page, the following left hander is usually blank. Text, and that's what the important central portion of your book is properly named, begins about half way down on the following right hand page which in this book is numbered 7, with continuing pages being 8, 9, 10, etc. Should front matter end on a left hand page, as our's did, it's okay to begin your book's text on the facing right hand page. The first text page does not carry the name of the book but it does bear the chapter title and page number such as the style of this book.

Somewhere along the line, book-production printers providing preliminary bids should have told you how many pages there are to each press signature. This is the big sheet of paper they use for printing books of common sizes. Press signatures are machine-folded down into specific page sizes ranging from 4, 8, 16, 32 or 64 book pages per sheet. For example: An 8-page signature for 5-1/2- by 8-1/2-inch books can be printed on an 11- by 17-inch press. It would print four pages on one side of an 11- by 17-inch sheet of paper and four on the other. When folded twice you would have an eight page signature. If this is confusing, fold a letter-size piece of paper into 1/4 sections. You will have eight pages measuring 4-1/4 by 5-1/2-inches. This example of a signature relates to the cost of producing a book. If your printer plates for 16- or 32-page signatures, and you have a book with 97 pages, you are running six 16-page signatures, or three 32-page signatures, for the first 96 pages of your book.

Front And Back Matter

Plus paying dearly for that single page (the 97th) which must be printed separately, run on a smaller press or whatever, which causes trouble for the printer and costs extra money for you. Do everything possible to design a book that comes out even as to the number of pages related to size of press signatures. Fill additional pages to make a 97-page book into a 108-page book or delete and combine material to cut a page out and reduce the book to 96 pages which is three 32's or six 16's or twelve 8's.

All of which is reason enough I strongly recommend that you determine what size signatures each of your bidding book-production printers would use for the proximate size book you are planning. With this information you can format your package to fit specific press equipment and in the doing keep costs to a minimum and profits at a pleasant maximum.

Our next move is to input the complete and sequenced Table of Contents (TOC) into the computer while omitting chapter page numbers. You'll insert chapter page numbers later, after you have a satisfactory book with all adjustments and inserts completed. At this time print out only the front matter and the numberless TOC so you have a fix on the number of book pages required up to the opening body text on a right-hand page. Please keep in mind; as front-matter page count changes so does total number of pages for the entire book. Once you have page count for the front matter and page count for the text you know precisely how many total pages remain free for back matter. Confusing? Perhaps, but what we're doing is establishing a profitable book wherein page control is critical. For example, suppose front matter uses seven pages and text absorbs 180. You now have a 187 page book with an available 192 pages if your book production printer plans to run six 32 page signatures. Deduct 187 from the 192 and you have five open pages remaining for the Index, References and other material. Need more space, jump four pages to a 196 page book, eight pages to a 200 page book or whatever your budget and market can handle.

While we're at this bit of additional material, there's also what is known as Back Matter which begins on right-hand pages. Back Matter may include, in this sequence; the Appendix, Special Notes, Glossary if your book requires one, References, Bibliography, and the Index. It's worth keeping in mind that if your book is to be valued as a reference work, length and completeness of the index is one of the strongest selling points you have. Make it good. The References section is second most important. The rest of back matter is only important as it supports usefulness of your package. Back matter may be printed in a type size slightly smaller than used for text. This saves space and sets the information off as an entity separate from the text.

References and business resources are a valuable asset to any self-published non-fiction book because they aid readers in furthering their knowledge or finding unusual support materials. There's not too many in this book because the publishing industry is highly volatile. Names and addresses are as changeable as the weather. Be that as it may, I've included a variety of the most useful to make your self publishing less troublesome. There's also the matter of a glossary. If your book is somewhat technical, add one. I have a small glossary to cover basics and help you do a better job of communicating with suppliers.

The Index, which always begins on a right hand page, is the difference between a mediocre and a great non-fiction book. Readers seek information and everything you can do to help it be found is a plus. Besides; savvy book buyers carefully consider the quality and depth of an index before deciding to plunk down their dollars.

As of now all separate chapter files, which are formatted as they will appear in your book, should be merged into one big file representing the entire book. Now use the publishing program's index feature, if it has one, by indexing every single thing the reader might like to find. Here are samples of the good and the bad in indexes which samples are intended only as friendly reminders to do better.

Eating Dog............21 (Look under "E" for a dog?)
Dog, Eating...........21 (Here's how to find it.)
Women's Dreams..39 (Check "W" for dreams?)
Dreams, Women's.39 (This will work.)

Front And Back Matter

Should the previous leave you a bit confused, open a good book and review the index closely. Your publishing program may offer a number of Index formats or you may want to create your own special style after inspecting the competition.

A word of caution. Do not program or hand index until the final, final, final printout of your book. Every format change or copy revision affects the index and you could be wasting time and effort if you index too early. This warning may not apply if your publishing program re-indexes automatically All you need do is push a few keys and relax as it reviews and updates page changes in program re-indexing.

As promised, here's a method of doing the Index by hand. It's not too difficult. Find that big yellow pad which should have enough (26) empty pages left. Letter the first clean page with a big fat "A" left-most on the bottom line. The next page gains a "B" on its bottom line with the "B" placed slightly to the right of the "A" location on the preceding page. Continue adding the alphabet from left to right until you have it spread along the bottom line of all 26 pages. Now it's easy to find a specific alphabet letter by fanning the pages. Read through your book after it has been formatted in the final design and printed out in sequence from page 1 to whatever. Select your index entries as you read the text. Log each index word and page number on its alpha yellow page, such as "Apples...23" on the "A" page, and "Zithers...147" on the "Z" page. Continue indexing the entire book by listing each entry and page number on its appropriate (A, B, C, etc.) yellow sheet. Your listings are not in any order, so we'll organize them with your computer's "sort" program. Type your index in the same format as the rest of the book with each listing on a separate line. Use the program's "Sort" function to place lines in alphabetical order based on your A-word to Z-word entries. If you are going to have a two-column index, sort it first as a single column then reformat the single column pages into two-columns per page for the final laser printout to paper.

In the time-consuming "I don't have a computer" department you may even have to do all sorting by hand. Here's how. Begin alphabetizing the "A" and other sheets as we did above. Read through your book after it has been formatted in the final design and printed out in sequence from page 1 to 180 or whatever. Select your index entries as you read the text. Log each index word and page number on its alpha yellow page, such as "Apples...23" on the "A" page, and "Zithers...147" on the "Z" page. Continue indexing the entire book by listing each entry and page number on its appropriate (A, B, C, etc.) yellow sheet. Then number each entry line in its the corrected alphabetical order such as (1) Absolutes...89, (2) Accuracy...27, (3) Admire...31, etc. Copy the alphabetized yellow sheet of "A"s in the new numeric sequence. After "A" is completed go to "B" and on to the rest of the list. Sounds dreadful, but other than being a somewhat slow process it is not all bad.

Front And Back Matter

In a non-fiction work the larger the index the more salable the book. Should your index comes up on the small side, consider larger print to make it more readable and appear larger. On the other hand if it is much too long, reformat the index into two columns or reduce the size of type.

When your book's total page count continues to be too long to fit your desired package or budget, consider a really tight editing. This removes details which on second thought the reader may not need for clear understanding of your message. This approach is fairly useful because tightening the package often makes information more quickly accessible. In addition you can again use your computer's format program to adjust text pages with even smaller type, more lines on each page or narrower margins to allow longer lines. However well these techniques work, keep in mind that such steps affect the book's perceived value. In the end you may be better off to spend a few more dollars for additional pages and make the book more appealing to your distributor and bookseller's potential market for books of your subject.

Making additional adjustments at this late date begins with using a long chapter as a test section to do type point-size adjustments, lines per page and line length things. If you're content with such changes as they affect appearance and value, go ahead and do all chapters the same way. Result, a newly formatted book that suits your budget and market niche objectives. Plus additional problems with new orphans and widows to fix and a TOC to be updated with revised page numbers. Hopefully the Index program works well and will automatically update itself when you run it all over again.

Now and then a book, in spite of all efforts, fails to fill the desired number of pages to be effectively competitive. Here it's reverse English. Larger type, wider margins for shorter lines and fewer lines per page. Such changes also affect the TOC, page formatting and the index. None of these will have much effect on potential purchasers of your book. What will affect shoppers negatively is opting to publish with so few pages your book seems undernourished when compared to competition on the bookseller's shelves. Obviously, for a mail-order package the latter point is not too important and may well reduce postage costs a considerable amount.

The References section of any book is best when reasonably complete with modest attention to material not directly related to the subject of your self-published book but which may be of more than passing interest and value to your reader. For example: A book on knitting could well direct readers to backup references on yarn dying, thermal properties of materials, knitting needles from around the world or garment sizing in areas outside the United States. All such subjects could be interesting though none are needed to learn knitting from a book. Use your best judgment here with two basic objectives in mind. One is to maximize your book by adding perceived value for the reader's benefit. The other is to provide expansive or unexpected benefits for the reader. With free space (extra pages) go for it. Otherwise proceed with caution for excessive material of marginal value to the reader increases cost of production and reduces your profit. That's important because we're *Self-Publishing Made Easy* and being successful is our objective.

Business resources could include Federal Agencies, association names and addresses and whatever important resources you find in library books devoted to such things. Trade publications may contain references related to the subject of your writing. Those included with this book are but a sampling of material in the field of book publishing.

Now is a very good time to take a break while you write for a Library of Congress Cataloging in Publication (LC) number; if they will give you one. In times past self-publishers were not able to obtain this number which is used as a reference point by public and private libraries. Be not too expectant. The Library's address is in the "References" section of this book. Also take steps to obtain an International Standard Book Number (ISBN). Contact R.R.Bowker at 1-888-269-5372 or check your potential book distributor for assistance. The "must do" is to obtain the copyright application Form TX. They're free and the address is, as you have guessed, in the back of this book with other related reference material supporting your self-publishing.

Front And Back Matter

Should such technical details as Front Matter, Back Matter, ISBN and LC numbers continue to be a bit confusing, take a moment to inspect the Front Matter and Back Matter pages of *Self-Publishing Made Easy*. Each of this book's early and late pages may be matched to the comments above with a few suggestions left for your imagination.

It's worth repeating that if you continue to have size problems at this time, the success key is simply to continue reformatting only one complete sample chapter until you get it right. I can't say it enough: "Controlling book production costs is critical for profit." Spend extra time here and continue evaluating adjustment results before selecting a final-final format. This being the laser printout which you will then be reviewing for brand new widows and orphans to repair. We fix these in yet another proofing explained in the following chapter wherein you make doubly certain the package is perfectly ready to be printed and published.

The next job to be completed in self-publishing is fine-tuning your design package. This is important to insure that your book reflects a quality appearance and arrives in your garage or closet inventory at the lowest reasonable cost.

Proofing To Print

After sweating the squeezing of creative juices through the sieves of my preceding chapters, and making dozens of unusual and critical interlocking decisions, laser printing the book in final form is a breeze. Front matter should be complete and perfect at this point, with the TOC not yet displaying chapter location page numbers. What follows is those decisions wherein attention to detail is important because some changes may affect the location of a chapter's first page.

What to do now is create and finalize, exactly what the printer will manufacture, buyers inspect and readers read.

Proofing To Print

Early on we did all the front matter, created a TOC and proofed a draft of a book in the format you desired. Then indexed it with a computer program but did not index it by hand because that later method must be last of the last. References and collateral material were inserted and you now have, in effect, an almost complete book: Minus the binding.

Here's the bad. Among adjustments you may be forced to make for this final laser printing could be changing the location of a page. For example; if you killed a widow on Page 60 you now have a blank page. All text following will automatically move forward one page to fill the blank which means all following pages will be identified one number lower. Which of course tilts index listings, the TOC and automatically convinces you that nothing can be done right. The sneaky way to keep from creating such escalating problems is not to kill the widow. Write enough extra text to partially fill the affected page and make it look good. Another area to check is the lower right and upper left corners of all text pages. Look for hyphenated words that begin on one page and have the other portion of the word on the next page. The easy fix is to insert spaces between words, or adjectives, preceding the hyphen area until you kick its first part over to join the second part on the following page.

Feel not badly as you find occasional misspellings or similar errors while scanning book pages. Perfect we're not. Such errors are easy to fix until you learn that some publishing programs cannot print out a single page and insist on printing out a chapter-full of pages just to output a single correction in the computer file. If you face this problem, the cure is "cut and paste" the old-fashion way. For example: On finding that "dog" should have been "cat" go to any printout of your book and find the word "cat." Carefully cut the word out with a razor or art knife and with equal care paste it over "dog." Bingo, you solved the problem and did not print out the entire chapter. But do revise the computer file on the off chance you could reprint a successful book later. Cut and paste works well for a word or two but it's not such a good technique if you find a dozen or so correx to be made. It's your call.

As we've traveled to this point I've mentioned artwork and detailed its formatting as related to location in the manuscript. text and chapter. Now we're going to get down and dirty into the hard work. Which is the skill of placing illustrations and photographs into open white spaces on the book's pages and, more importantly, near related text.

No illustrations or photographs ?

Skip this section and fast-forward.

Black and white photos reproduced inside a book on text pages are super sales agents. Buyers often fan a book for photos and buy without reading a word of the text. Color pictures do it even better. The given being that all such photographic material should have an informative caption beneath it to explain things the viewer cannot observe in the picture. Check major picture magazines for the techniques of caption writing. Notice what the caption says, and what it does not say, about each illustration. Caption writing is an art in itself, a talent far different than writing paragraph after paragraph of book text. Go slow and do the best you can.

Among quality photographic artists and color separators who prepare screened negatives for printing color pictures on paper, there is firm agreement that color printing reproduced from transparencies, such as slides, is superior to color printing from other common color sources including photo prints. However, and that's a big "however," reproductions from photo prints are about 95 percent as good as reproductions from transparencies. The short story being that for books the use of color prints as the basis of reproductions is dandy and works almost as well as transparencies. Save money when specifying the source of your color reproductions. The surface of book paper and speed of book printing presses makes superior quality of a transparency almost redundant. They are really too good for the printing process of the average self-published book. All bets are off in this area if your book is an art work where accurate color reproduction is essential to success of the book. Stock photos on CDs, from the internet, can be satisfactory if their resolution is high enough. Ask your printer for instructions on making use of material from these rapidly changing low-cost sources of color photography.

Proofing To Print

This worry area of art insertion actually began when you were writing the text and I suggested that you insert a line for each piece of artwork (charts, graphs, line drawings, etc.) you though might be necessary. That notation was in all capitals (ART 9-A 4-1/2") on a separate line between paragraphs. Then as you began to modify the book into its press-ready format I had you insert a sufficient number of line spaces to create a blank area or "window" of the desired size (4-1/2", etc.) into which the artwork would be inserted.

One procedure for inserting photographs and artwork into your book is to send the original art to the printer along with the press-ready pages of the book which have open windows amid the appropriate text. Attached to or marked on each piece of art should be a notation as to the page number and specific location on the page: Such as Page 9-A which calls for the graphic to be located on page 9 in the open window (the area in which there is no text) marked by you as A. Easy. No work for you and the printer is responsible for doing it right. Hard, because this is the most expensive way possible. However this procedure is the only practical way for the small publisher to handle the insertion of color photographs or art into a book. The drill boils down to laying out the pages with windows for the artwork. The printer places the artwork in place and then sends you a proof of the book so you can decide if Aunt Emma's picture really belongs with the chapter on animal husbandry or coal mining.

Proofing To Print

Much less expensive and equally effective for black and white photographs is the use of screened prints, or "Veloxes" as they were called in the far distant past. To obtain screened prints or good reproduction quality copies look in the telephone book for the category of "Lithographic Plates & Negatives." This business listing is for firms who specialize in the production of quality copies ("repros") or screened paper prints for paste-up. If that listing's not to be found look for "Lithographers" who are more often than not printers. They may or may not provide screened print services but should be able to refer you to someone who does make quality prints at reasonable cost. A screened print is simply a paper print reproduction of a photograph or continuous tone art which has been pre-screened so the print bears the half-tone dot pattern required for book printing. The book production printer can photograph a page bearing both text and screened prints on one piece of litho film from which the plate is made. There is no extra charge by the printer for doing fine-line negatives this way.

For drawings or charts (art) you'll only need high quality copies. These are not made by office copy machines. A reproduction-quality copy of line art is simply a top-quality paper print which will reproduce perfectly in your book. Not expensive if you have such copies made locally and paste the print on the page adjacent to its text. As a side note, such screened and reproduction prints are usually made by what is called the "PMT" process. A screened print is described as a

"PMT Half-Tone" and the print of a drawing or chart may be termed a "PMT Line Reproduction." The litho cameraperson shoots the art on sheet of photosensitive paper. It is placed against a reception sheet then passed through a chemical bath and between rubber rollers. After a minute or so the two sheets are separated. The reception sheet carries the photo or art image which, when dry, is pasted into position on the text page.

Should you have a high-quality scanner you too can scan the black and white art or photograph and screen it with the number of lines per inch (LPI) requested by the printer. ie: Scan at 100 LPI. Print this scanned image at the maximum DPI (Dots Per Inch) through your laser printer on the best quality laser printing paper you can find.

There are professional quality scanners and laser printers which could allow you to make negatives for the book production printer's use. These procedures are highly technical and subject to time-wasting problems for the unpracticed. I'd suggest you not bother with doing negatives until you have plenty of time for a months-long learning curve. This training period should include extensive cooling-off sessions to reduce stress, frustration and door-slamming as you go for fresh coffee and aspirin.

After trimming a screened print to exact size, paste it into the open window amid the text. Office supply stores have useful temporary adhesive tape procedures which work well. This is the same procedure you would use if the screened print were supplied by the Lithographic Negative and Plate service. Using screened prints could not be easier. Just be careful to trim the prints with horizons and buildings as true verticals or horizontals. Tilted art, or photographs, in any book shows badly on completion.

In the Computer To Press (CTP) technology, wherein you send the printer your book on a computer disk, the art is scanned, the image screened then mouse-moved into position on your computer monitor's image of the page. Click on the SAVE button and combined art and page will be preserved on a disk with all the rest of your book. Run off a laser printer proof of what you have done to be sure all is well and that's the end of it. The book production printer will use your disk to transfer your entire book, text and art, onto the press plate and the printing press does the rest. There are too many computer programs in this field for any specific procedure to be included here. Follow the publishing or graphics-handling program instructions to get the job done to suit your book design format. It's fairly easy after you try a few dozen times.

At this point you should have every chapter chained in a merged file on a single disk with a backup collection of the merged files on another floppy. Start with Chapter 1 and check each page on the monitor for just two things. Did you miss fixing any widows or orphans? If the complete file of your book passes inspection use the best laser printing paper stock you can find and print it out in the final/book format. I use

Proofing To Print

80 lb. matte paper in 8-1/2 by 11-inch size. It sails through a HP printer running 300 DPI (Dots To Inch) that was tricked into producing 600 DPI output. With whatever paper stock you use, go for a heavy toner setting to give you quality output for two copies of the entire book. Run all the pages at the same time to eliminate the possibility of outputting sheets which vary from light to dark from one laser printing session to the other. Wrap and hide one copy of the printout in a secure place. Use the remaining copy for an additional late-evening review and opportunity to catch those sneaky typographical errors (typos) and occasional glaring error of fact or sequence. Inspect page numbers for accuracy and check them against the TOC, verify a random selection of Index entries and review the printed sheets (again) for widows and orphans. In case we skipped a beat here, this top quality final printout will be used to produce negatives and plates from which your book will be printed. The same set of computer disk files could also be Postscript merge-printed to a second disk for use in a POD, CTP or DTP process you may have considered using.

Books of many pages sometimes overwhelm the best computer's program. Break the book into sections of about 100 pages each. Each chapter must start with its page number in sequence and all will be well.

We began this chapter on the subject of illustrations and photographs then ended with a complete book ready for publication. The next section moves into controlling out-of-pocket dollars.

Paper Stock Selection

With the price of paper affecting about half of the cost of printing a book, it's well worth a chapter by itself to help you consider available options before deciding on the text-paper specification of your book.

Least expensive would be printing a book on newspaper stock, with which you already have a considerable amount of experience. It tears easily, reproduces photos badly and ages rapidly into crumbles. At the other end of the spectrum is paper hand-made by craftsmen who create sheets of exquisite beauty. Like all hand-made goodies such papers are enormously expensive and not really so well suited for books as they are for impressive brochures or wake and let's-party invitations.

Paper Stock Selection

At the practical level exists a broad product spectrum the trade describes as "Book Papers." They are manufactured specifically to meet the best parameters of book printing. Their special qualities include weight as related to thickness, ability to fold without tearing, opacity, surface treatment and resistance to color deterioration over time.

Let's review the critical characteristics.

Book paper specifications begin with "weight." A 30# (30-pound) stock is somewhat heavier than that sold in office supply stores as typewriter paper. At the other end is 100# text stock which is thick and impressive. Thin is usually low in cost unless you specify "Bible paper" which is not cheap. Thick is expensive. Thinner papers are useful in situations where you must have a great number of pages but wish to keep your book's thickness (bulk) to a reasonable size. Telephone books and Bibles are good examples of this form of text paper. Thick pages are useful when you are short of words but want the book to be fat enough to make a favorable impression. Most-used text weights range from 30# (thin) to 60# or 70# which are pleasantly thick. Paper manufacturers provide a thickness specification such as 350 ppi, or 465 ppi, which translates to 350 pages per inch or 465 pages per inch. Using this simple specification provides the essential information as to how impressive your book and its spine width will be when stacked on the bookseller's shelves. Competitive books are a good indication of what is average. Your selection of paper

Paper Stock Selection

weight and quality will come off best as a considered decision balanced to meet specific sales objectives and the expense of printing the desired number of books.

A low cost way to fatten a book is to use speciality text papers known as "bulking stock" which are light in weight but slightly thicker than their weight designation would normally indicate. A 50# weight bulking book stock has the thickness and feel near a typical 70# stock but it is usually less durable. You will find these specification differences in the 50# X-Bulk stock listed in the following chart. Bulking stock is manufactured by aerating the pulp mixture with the result that you have a rather porous paper which does not reproduce photography well. But it's another option that has value in making a text book thicker than it would be if printed on regular paper. To rephrase this, with bulking stock a book of 150 pages could be as thick as a book with 225 pages printed on regular book stock. And in the book business, thickness is often perceived by the shopper as value. Use the paper specification of sheets per inch (ppi) to compare possible book thickness before deciding on the best for your market.

On the next page is a list of papers that one printer keeps on hand at all times. Note the many differences of thickness, weight and surface.

Paper Stock Selection

Typical Selection of Floor Sheets

	PPI	Sheet Size	Opacity	Comments
50# Husky Smooth Offset 550ppi		35x45	90	Blue white
50# Husky Smooth Offset 550ppi		38x50	90	Popular
50# Husky Smooth Offset 550ppi		41x56	90	
60# Husky Smooth Offset 424ppi		35x45	92	
60# Husky Smooth Offset 424ppi		38x50	92	
50# Glatfelter X-Bulk	360ppi	35x45	92	Natural
50# Glatfelter X-Bulk	360ppi	38x50	92	Popular
50# Glatfelter X-Bulk	360ppi	41x56	92	Rough
50# Finch Opaque Smooth 606ppi		35x45	94	Opaque
50# Finch Opaque Smooth 606ppi		38x50	94	Popular
50# Finch Opaque Smooth 606ppi		41x56	94	
60# Finch Opaque Smooth 500ppi		35x45	93	
60# Fortune Galaxie	714ppi	35x45	77	Low cost
60# Raptor Gloss	740ppi	35x45	92	Popular
60# Raptor Gloss	740ppi	23x35	92	
70# Raptor Gloss	570ppi	35x45	93	
70# Raptor Gloss	570ppi	23x35	93	
60# Porcelain Gloss	740ppi	35x45	88	
60# Porcelain Gloss	740ppi	23x35	88	
70# Porcelain Gloss	645ppi	35x45	89	
70# Porcelain Gloss	645ppi	23x35	89	
60# Patina Matte	626ppi	35x45	92	
60# Patina Matte	626ppi	23x35	92	
70# Premier Matte	460ppi	35x45	95	
8 pt. C1S Cover				
8 pt. C2S Cover				
10 pt. C1S Cover				
12 pt. C1S Cover				

Floor Sheet List courtesy of Capital City Press, Montpelier, VT 05601

Self Publishing Made Easy

Paper Stock Selection

Another area of decision is color of the text stock. Almost every imaginable color is available, with your book-production printer being the initial source of sample sheets. Colored paper seldom costs a great deal more than white which makes it usable at reasonable cost. On the other hand, when you decide on white the story is wild. For book text stock termed "white" you will find hundreds of sheets, the whiteness of which ranges all over the block. There is gray white, blue white, yellow white, white white, cold white, warm white and tons of others. A careful inspection of samples will disclose their color differences of which the major factor is cost. An "off white" paper is one that was produced with a bare minimum of bleaching chemicals or white fillers which reduces the cost of production. You pay a bit less and settle for less white than a more expensive whiter white. At the other end of the spectrum are whites so white they hurt the eyes. These are manufactured with heavy bleaching to eliminate natural coloration of their wood or fabric base, then filled and/or coated with the finest of clays to fill pores and present a virginal appearance. Again, cost is the determining factor. The less perfect, the less cost; with your eye and budget being the final determiner of the appearance your book should present to the potential or actual buyer.

Opacity is a term describing the ability of a book paper to prevent printing on one side of the sheet from showing through on the other side of the sheet. Back to the telephone book and Bible. Their thin papers are carefully manufactured to control opacity, though in most instances there may be a modest and acceptable show-through of printing. It's needful to report that in some instances an inexpensive thick paper (60# or 70#) could allow ink to bleed from one side of the sheet to the other. In this situation you could have show-through even though the stock is thick. Opacity is a specific area where you should have a printed sample of the desired text stock to assure yourself that its opacity is all you desire. In sample books from paper manufacturers, inspect the backside of their sheets for show-though of paper weight identification data printed on the front side. Another test is to letter on a sample with a black ball-point or brush pen then inspect the other side for color show-through.

Surface texture of book paper is established at the mill on both sides of the sheet. This compares to cover stock which will often be produced with a different surface on each side. In simple terms, book paper is usually considered as having a glossy surface, a vellum surface or a matte surface. The glossy surface reproduces text and art with the greatest clarity, and remains clean longer. The vellum surface appears somewhere between glossy and matte. It reproduces well and is often used where a quality-oriented appearance is desired. Matte surface book paper, most of all in the 70# or 80# weights, is great for coffee-table books with good art reproductions. It also presents a good "feel" of quality as you turn the pages. Amid surface specifications there are both coated and uncoated stocks. The coated matte stock presents something of a glarefree surface but has enough minerals pressed into the surface to improve reproduction of halftones and color. Uncoated stock is, as the name implies, matte paper without such technical additions.

Overall dimensions of the base sheet can be very important in costing a book. If you, the publisher, select a sheet texture which is only manufactured in an overall dimension larger or smaller than the most efficient printing press, your production costs will increase. When the sheet is larger you will be charged for the full sheet though the book printer trims it down to fit his press and throws the trimmings away. On the other hand, if the sheet you desire is too small for the most efficient press, the job will take longer to run on a less capable or smaller press which is going to add cost to your printer's invoice. Printers selected to provide a final RFQ will usually tell you of the undersize sheet and may ignore the oversize paper specification. Should your bidder be running small web presses, you'll find text paper choices to be severely limited. This is because web presses print from rolls of paper and roll stock is not released in a wide variety of surfaces and weights. Most important of all web restrictions is that if you decide on an uncommon paper weight, the printer is not going to be happy about purchasing an entire roll for a run that will only use a portion of the roll. You may be able to dicker with the printer in this area by offering to accept a complete roll run which could be 843 books or 1289; instead of insisting he produce only an exact 500 or 1000.

Availability of product also adversely affects your paper selection. Should you have decided on a stock not generally available, and the mill has none in inventory, you may wait for months before your selection comes off the production line. To this delay must be added time for the books to be printed.

So what to do?

Begin with competitive books begged, bought or borrowed during your market research activities. When you find text paper you can be happy with, send a sample page to each book production printer at the time you ask for an RFQ. Add a side note explaining that if they do not have that specific stock, they should bid on the nearest comparable in-house stock ("floor sheet") which matches, and send you a sample of that floor sheet with their bid. After samples arrive you can evaluate weight and color by comparison. For opacity testing use a ball point or brush pen to write on both a page of the competitive book and on the sample substitute sheet provided by the printer. Show-through should be about the same for both papers. You luck out when the book-production printer has a sheet you really like and will sell it to you at his bulk-purchase price. If not, telephone the printer for something else. More samples could be forthcoming for your consideration and speculation.

For fancy textures, colors or papers of thickness; the best thing to do is send samples of what you like and request a telephone response. Then you can tell the sales rep what it is you want to accomplish so that he or she may be able to suggest other and/or less expensive ways to reach your objective. You're on your own in this area as unusual paper stock is expensive and usually difficult to obtain at the precise time you want it.

How critical all these factors are to the book design is up to you. For the most part, none of them are considered very important for a mail-order item. The "if" factor compares a commercial product vs. a prestige product. It's your book and by balancing available dollars and intended use, vs. the book market, you can make self-publishing much more successful and far less stressful.

The final point on this paper bit is that paper manufacturers provide charts and sample books of their products without charge. To obtain stock sample books, check the yellow pages for Paper Wholesalers and call around to their Order Desks.

After text paper decisions are made, there's more. You need a cover; its design, colors, stock on which it will be printed, surface protection and method of binding around the book. All being areas I'll move into with the following chapter.

Book Covers

If preceding final adjustments seemed complicated, relax.

Here is the most demanding area of self publishing.

The cover.

Should you not be comfortable with that two-word specification, reflect on what you observed while doing market research in book stores. I submit that the first thing to catch your eye was the cover or spine of shelved books. Which says it all. When seeking book store sales your cover has to be as good or better than anything you observed or bought for inspection and consideration of emulation.

Book Covers

Reason(s) enough for the multitude of cover decisions. These include choice of a paper (stock) on which it will be printed, color of the stock, color(s) of ink, location of the UPC code, art work or photograph(s), type font, method of binding, title supportive front-cover text to sell the book, continuation of sales text onto the outside back cover, what text prints inside front and back covers and words of the highly important headline that prints on the spine. Remember, the spine is the first (and often only) thing a book browser sees while eyeballing bookstore shelves. This tiny slice of space is a most demanding area for your initial sales pitch.

Skipping back to the time you spent cruising book stores for comparable books, reconsider that as you walked past the shelves you saw more spines than covers. If a spine caught your eye, you pulled the book for inspection. As you may recall, some spines were displaying type so small it was almost unreadable. Other spines told you little or nothing about the book's subject or theme. The easy answer to such diversity is to consider text on the spine as a newspaper headline. If it makes you eager to take the book down (read the story) it is a good headline and an even better spine. A poor headline (spine) and you would pass it. This is where a fat book has the advantage of impressive size which is one of several reasons why more pages, or thick paper (bulking stock) may well be worth paying for. The trade-off is spending money for advertising room on the spine or not being overly conspicuous.

Book Covers

It's not all wrong to pay good money to a cover-design specialist to do the cover for you if bookseller shelves are your objective. It's that important. On the other hand, if you're producing a mail-order package the cover is of modest importance. The cover design area of book production is defined as "Proceed at your own risk." And pray a lot.

It is generally considered by printers that you should leave about one-quarter inch of free space around all art and copy designed inside the cover's trim line. This clear space is enough additional area for the sheet of paper to be kissed by the ink rollers. Printers also need a bit of extra margin for the book binding operation where a sixteenth of an inch shortage can be a problem. In plain english; if text and art are too close to the edge they could be cut off in the printing or binding process. However there's what is called "bleed" text and art. It prints right up to and over the edge of the cover. This is planned during design of the cover. Printers recommend a minimum of 1/8" allowance for trim of bleed pages or covers. You have, no doubt, seen many books with this type of cover layout in which art ran off the edge of the paper. The catch is important. Bleed printing is more expensive because extra wide/long paper stock may be needed and paper stock costs money when it exceeds standard sizes. While bleeds are impressive, they cost. In cover layout you are well advised to balance the additional cost vs. the added presentation value you perceive in a bleed arrangement. Competitive books

Book Covers

will help you to help make an informed decision about showing better than the best in your intended market.

For a self publisher making a cover layout is great fun because you are encouraged to play God. With a soft pencil and blank sheet of paper, on which the final cover size is indicated by border lines, you can move title, copy and art around the world to suit yourself. My usual practice is to draw as many cover roughs as my mind conjures then spread them all over the dining-room table. As time passes I'll review them again and again, turning over those which, under continuing consideration, fail to meet standards for a ten-foot cover that sells. Finally I'll be down to two or three for careful evaluation or conversion into laser printed samples. You can produce headlines, art and text on the laser printer and paste them into position on the cover the same way you would paste screened and repro prints in the text section of your book. Because this is so simple, I often paste up the final few cover roughs for day-long consideration. It's an easy way to make better decisions.

A recent report on book covers detailed a few key points of cover design. It's easily agreed that many pulp books on news stands display covers created to hit shoppers so hard they'll open the book to see what all the commotion is about. For sure this is one way to sell books. And it works. On the other hand, understating is considered the best way to market the self-help or how-to book. Other considerations include the book that is undersize, such as 3 by 5 inches or 5 by 3 inches. The rationale is simple. With 80% of book store sales to women, it's easy to design for a woman to buy and purse a small odd-size book such as one that is wide or narrow. As artists will explain, design and art on a cover can be highly impactive. A square shape is considered to be a solid and stable object. A round shape one that can roll or move. Curves are soft and gentle, lines and angles aggressive. Nature, with greens and blues, denotes peace and harmony. Deep clouds and stormy seas the exact opposite. If you're a bit lost in this area take time to review the wealth of magazine advertising pages and from them learn how art and design supports (or in some instances, destroys) the product message. It's a wide-open field for your artistic innovation and creativity.

After your cover has been laid out and you have a good idea of where title, art and credits go, you'll be faced with the daunting task of writing advertising copy. Words printed on the cover are the best shot you will ever have to get the browser/shopper to open your book or buy it unopened. This is one very good reason to write the cover copy 20 times and then do it all over again until you have the most powerful collection of prose you can write. Should you like guidance, take time to very thoroughly analyze the copy in a mail-order catalog. Some of it is so good you can't wait to order something. Other copy is so bad you wonder how they remain in business. To repeat, what's on your cover is the best shot to sell your book. The spine must get shoppers to take your book off the shelf but words on the cover complete the selling job. Unless, of course, you have written a book so widely controversial and publicized that shoppers buy without consideration.

Colored cover stock is only slightly more expensive than white, which in itself comes in that previously discussed great variety of whites: Blue-white, yellow-white, grayed-white and a couple hundred variations in between. You can make good use of any white cover stock by printing a background color overall with the title reversed out by the paper's white surface. Some books you have inspected may have used this technique which is fairly low in cost. The catch is precisely spelling out for the book-production printer, how thick (10% to 90%) you want color laid onto the cover as a background. Find something you really like, use it for your sample and include this specification, "Background Color To Sample Provided," on your purchase order. The bottom line being that color has the reputation of improving sales. Colored stock is one way, color printing is another, reversing the type out to white inside a color background is another and there's a few oddballs, such as cutouts or embossing, that cost extra money and are most impressive. Here again, inspect what others are doing and use the very best you can find and/or afford.

There's also the matter of glossy, matte or textured stock and quality of the cover material. Sample books are the best source of guidance here. Find things you like and talk to your printer's rep about costs as compared to the image desired for your book. A real eyeball catcher is the use of bright foil stamping on portions of the cover. You'll find a lot of this on food-store paperbacks. Such foils are usually manufactured in layers which include a polyester film carrier, color coat, metal (aluminum) in metallic foils, and the dry adhesive that makes the piece stick in place. Costs for such treatment begin with $50 to $3000 for a basic die. A piece of foil is laid over the cover and the heated die is stamped down onto the foil. The adhesive is activated by the heat and you have a unique cover. In addition to basic cost of the cover, foil stamping adds from a dime on up depending on how many covers are run at one time. Not all book production houses offer this service. Those who do not usually have a vendor to provide foil stamping.

Technical stuff presented along the bottom lower edge of the back cover includes UPC code bars in the Bookland format, the ISBN number of your book and its sales price. It's helpful to add a line as to where in the bookstore it should be shelved. Such as: Reference, Cooking, Travel or whatever designated location you learned during market research suggested in my chapter titled "The Competition."

The ISBN number is available from the ISBN Agency, in New Jersey ("References") or through your book production facility. These numbers are strictly controlled and once you assign an ISBN number to a publication, the number should never be used again. The exception is when you reprint without changes and the original number can be repeated. Should you make text or cover changes, and in effect be creating a new edition, a new ISBN number is required. You'll find the ISBN for *Self Publishing Made Easy* on the outside of the back cover as 0-910390-63-0 just above the box of vertical UPC bars. The reason for that ugly panel of black lines is that it can be read by a scanner, as they do groceries, to provide both price and ISBN information. Most major book chains will not stock a book unless it bears the ISBN number and UPC code on the outside cover. Your book production printer may be able to provide UPC bar codes or you can find local vendors under the "Label" listing of the telephone book. There's also a trade organization, the Uniform Code Council, in References.

You may have noticed that many book covers are presented in which the title is in one color, selling text in another and perhaps line art in a third. The easy way to do this is to let the printer shoot each subject separately to size (title, text, art) and merge the films in his shop. This type of cover needs reasonably accurate production and is not overly expensive. You can also have this merging done at the local Photo/Litho shop we suggested you find in connection with screened prints and reproduction copies of drawings and charts. The cost may not be lower but you will be able to make good use of over-the-counter conversation to insure receiving exactly what you want or suggestions to do it better.

A low cost way is to do-it-yourself with help of your laser printer and clear laser-printable plastic sold by office supply stores in boxes of 25 or 50 letter-size sheets. Print only the title on one sheet. Print the selling text on another piece of plastic. And print art on a third sheet. Mark each piece of plastic as to the color you want, or attach a sample color patch clipped from a magazine. Then use masking tape to hinge top edges only, one over the other, with title, selling copy and art in the precise position you want them to appear on the cover. When laid up this way you can see how your cover will appear if everything were printed with black. The book-printer's camera people can burn (image) their printing plate negative from your clear plastic sheets. This is a bit more complicated than a short paragraph could cover so I recommend hitting the library for a book on the subject of "Mechanical Art Work." It will detail procedures with examples of each step of the process. Anyhow, this technique is recommended as being low in cost and easy to do once you have it figured out. Your selected book-production printer can guide you in providing the title, text and art to best fit his needs in the negative stripping room. Said printer will also suggest you let him take care of it for a few additional dollars on the bid. If you have any doubts about your skills, let the printer do it.

If you want to use color pictures on the outside of your cover, please re-read pages of Chapter 16 "Proofing To Print" for a backgrounding on how color is best handled. The basics are to keep it simple. To establish a single point of responsibility for quality have the book printer do it all. In general, a four-color cover such as the reproduction of a photograph on the cover of your book, is printed by a press with four impression cylinders. As the cover stock passes through the press the first cylinder prints the yellow image, the second cylinder the red image, the third a blue/cyan image and the fourth cylinder prints the black image. The result is a print that reproduces, more or less, the colors of your original. As printing techniques improve, the order of laying colors is changing. Upgraded super-quality color printing is now done on presses fitted with more than four cylinders to lay down additional colors or a protective surface coating at one pass of paper through the press.

Cover protective finishes include UV coating, glossy lamination which brightens colors or matte lamination which dulls them. Such surface treatments are intended to keep your book from appearing shelf-worn over the period of time it is at the bookseller's. If you'd care for a recommendation, I suggest the UV (UltraViolet) anti-fade protection coating which is usually a no- or low-cost item when compared to lamination. The water-based UV coating is applied by a separate roller on the same press that prints the cover, therefore the printer's cost is near zero. It protects covers very well. Gloss or matte laminate is an additional operation and accordingly more expensive. Printers will usually supply samples of such services for your decision. The range is narrow so insist your selected print shop show you the options they provide. Important final point: Laminated covers often curl if exposed to sun or heat. Insist on "lay-flat" film if the protection your printer recommends, or only provides, is plastic lamination.

As a side note. In some instances the press and paper size required to run your cover will create a sizable amount of trim to be removed. Ask the printer about this one as you could use the trim to print, at the same time as your primary cover, a smaller cover for use as a homemade booklet or mailer. It's only cost will be additional "prep" work in film separation as press time and paper will be fixed by the primary cover.

Accordingly, use all the money you can afford to wrap the best possible cover around a book targeted for retail booksellers. Self-published books can rise and fall on their covers and titles. On the other hand, if you're planning mail-order sales the cover can be a happy plain Jane. In either area there's extra dollars to be gained by printing sales messages on the inside front and back covers to encourage the buying of your book or suggest mail orders for additional copies. It's free advertising space and you may as well use it. Most food-store paperbacks have an order form and book list in the back of the book. If it works for them, there's no reason why it can't work for you and result in additional orders.

By now I hope you've accepted my message.

Next to title and subject matter of your book, the cover is the most important sales tool you have. Now let's have a book printed at the most favorable cost.

The Best Printing Price

Printers, as individuals, are some of the nicest people I've met.

As businessmen/women they are the most stressed out, unreasonable, unreliable, inconsiderate, executives in the world. And for very good reasons. Competition in the printing business is open warfare with price-cutting the norm to keep equipment and staff busy. Presses now cost in the hundreds of thousands or millions of dollars; paper prices can and often do change daily, for the most part customers all want something different, good employees are almost impossible to find, and when the job is shipped everyone stops breathing while hoping the client (you) will be happy with the paper, ink, colors, delivery date, ultimate price and the book.

The Best Printing Price

The worst part is, to book-production printers, self-publishers are a pain. The print run is small, self publishers seldom generate repeat business, those who've not read *Self-Publishing Made Easy* won't know what they want or should have, and they usually require more hand-holding than a profitable print job from a consistent customer. Many large book printers maintain a special sales staff to handle self-publishers as a means of reducing stress on more experienced employees negotiating with major publishers.

You're being warned. Be prepared to negotiate thoughtfully, be not too pleased with the ongoing experience and know for a certainty that your books will never arrive precisely as promised. That's life...in the self-publishing business, and as follows, for major publishers as well.

This reads horribly negative and I apologize to those tender souls who are in the printing business or value a printer executive as friend or spouse. But there's more than personal opinion behind these negative comments. A recent report pointed out that trade book publishers change printers about 50 percent of the time because of poor quality or service, inability to meet delivery deadlines, dishonesty, lack of communications and price. It's worth noting that price was not the most stated reason for changing. Over 40% of the same surveyed group spoke of quality as being their prime concern as compared to less than 20% who considered price the most important. And a worrisome percentage of publishers change printers every year.

The Best Printing Price

There is great variation among book manufacturers, who I sometimes describe as printers to save typing, as more and more of the more reliable shops begin to specialize in niche markets. What is needed for profitable self-publishers is a printer of books. Which is simply a factory that specializes in the production of books. A few shops print only one size book, others will print any size you want. Some do everything through pre-press, camera work and binding, under their roof. Small shops purchase many services from outside vendors. The big boys buy paper by the carload and stock a few basic sheets and weights they sell to you at a price lower than the going market for a one-book lot of paper. Others buy paper as needed and pay the higher spot-market price, which extra cost is passed on to you. Some have great production specialists who can give you telephone information about your job at the drop of a hat. Other shops place voice-mail barriers in the way and make it almost impossible to find out what is happening to your book, or even if/when it will ever happen.

What works best is a specialist book printer who stocks paper you approve of, commonly prints and binds the size book you want, on his factory floor with the skills of his employees. Should there be none in your area contact editors of major printing magazines for their current listing of book manufacturing plants. The library has a massive volume listing printing magazines published in the U.S. A few of the majors are listed in the "References" section of this book.

The Best Printing Price

In sum finding a good place to have your book printed is easy or impossible depending on how you approach the problem. And that it is...a problem. Particularly if you fail to keep in mind that "printers" are not book manufacturers.

A good place to begin searching is with your peer group. Inquire closely of area publishers about their experiences with book production and printer recommendations. Ask about the book manufacturer's helpfulness in creating an economical package, integrity in keeping promises made, responsiveness to inquiries and delivery of a satisfactory product on or close to the agreed upon schedule. As you have noticed, price was not the most important thing. A low-cost book of poor quality won't sell. Because this is *Self Publishing Made Easy* the publication of a reasonably profitable book is our objective.

In this book's Reference section is a group of sources who can provide information on book manufacturing plants and a number of well-known book producers you could contact. Write to the groups for a list of their members and advertisers, then write to obtain bids from other book manufacturers who specialize in short runs of 500 to 10,000 books. Vendors who try hard to help you are a plus and will often produce the best books. Those who "ho hum" at another self-publisher are more than likely to either ignore you or make the relationship too difficult to enjoy. Preliminary bids that offer books a cost far below the average of all others may indicate a "low

The Best Printing Price

ball" printer. The usual manner of bidding an extremely low price is to specify a substitute paper that you do not want as a means of quoting lower than their competition. Other substitutions may be short-weight cover stock, smaller trim size and undesired bindery techniques. As you narrow the preliminary bid list down to two or three vendors, on the basis of overall cost including freight to your door, ask for a sample book matching your specifications. If they won't provide samples, cool it.

Ask questions. Then more questions. And more...until you're as full of answers as questioning skills produce.

One of the critical factors in costing a book, after selection of paper, is the press on which it will be printed. Though individual printers have their own "standard" sizes, here's a generic example of what is called a press "signature." In this instance the sheet of paper is 38- by 50-inches. On one pass through the press it will be printed on both sides. From that pass you could have 16 pages 9- by 12-inches, 48 pages 8- by 8-inches, 64 pages 6-1/8- by 9-1/4-inches, 96 pages 4-1/2- by 8-inches, 128 pages 4-1/2- by 6-inches or 96 pages in the 6- by 9-inch size. All these different book size pages would result from the manner in which that one 38- by 50-inch signature sheet was folded down. Accordingly by sizing your book to fit whatever "standard" trim sizes your printer offers you'll be doing what's possible to keep this portion of your costs in line. Select a non-standard size and you'll be paying for wasted paper or excess press time and labor. These are good reasons to thoughtfully consult with the printer's rep as to preferred book size.

Here's another emerging technique that could be of interest to new self-publishers. It's called printing on demand (POD). This procedure is becoming available from chain or large independent copy shops and through those many book printers and distributors who have moved into the field. You prepare the book on a computer disk somewhat as for CTP presentation to a book manufacturer. But you send the disk to an on-demand shop who can produce one, five or 100 completed books. The book's covers are printed digitally by a superior color laser printer and then laminated for appearance and protection. Yes, the price per book is high: Usually about triple the cost per copy from a more traditional book manufacturer producing 500 or 1000 copies at a time. If you've priced your book to sell at a profit though the unit cost is high, printing on demand reduces both total dollars of your investment at any one period and number of books taking up space in the garage. Besides, if you want to revise the book it's easy to make changes on the computer disk for another printing. Pop a "Revised Edition" sticker on the cover, add a new ISBN and like magic you have a new book. Printing on Demand is worth serious consideration if your cost/benefit ratio bottom-lines on the high side of profit per book. New procedures on the way will make it possible to print additional copies of the full-color covers which could be gloss-laminated to provide very attractive promotional inserts to travel with your publicity releases.

POD cost data provided by one reputable book production house reported that 100 copies of a 5-1/2 by 8-1/2-inch book of 224 pages on 50# text stock would cost about $2500 if printed in the usual manner on an offset press. The same 100 books printed on a digital (laser) machine would cost about $850. Sure, you save $1650 on printing those 100 copies. But the POD charge per book would be $8.50 each. Multiply this by the 1 to 5, or 1 to 8, pricing factor and that 224 page book would have to sell for anything from $42.50 to $68.00. Which appears to be well above the retail price of any similar package in the book trade. Another POD plant reported (in 1999) that a 300-page 6- by 9-inch book, with four-color cover would cost about $4.80 each in quantities of 25 or more books ordered at one time. At a 1 to 5 retail to cost ratio this book would sell for $25 which may be profitable for a self-publisher marketing through booksellers and mail order. POD is a service worth checking as its costs per book are likely to drop from the data provided about. It appears that up to about 300 copies, POD is economic. More than 300 could be less costly per book if run on a conventional offset press.

Sneaky stuff goes on when you're selling by mail. Delete the four-color covers and binding, and have the POD sheets come off the press collated in page sequence with punched holes for a three-ring binder or folder. You could hold print orders down to

The Best Printing Price

ten or 20 copies of the book at a time and stuff the binders or folders yourself. Full-color prints of photographs or art, to be inserted in the plastic sleeve on the front of the binder, are about 35 cents each in quantity. Or for a small book or booklet, go to self covers with staples to hold the thing together. It's also possible your print-on-demand or local copy shop will be able to do simple plastic, comb or perfect binding in small quantities to fill orders as you receive them.

From the emerging POD processes we should move to consideration of conventional book printing and the best equipment on which to print your package. For short runs of 500 to 5,000 books modern sheetfed presses are best. A single-color press is less expensive for the printer to buy and the cost per sheet of its time and labor is proportionately lower than running a black-ink book on a multi-color press designed and priced to print four colors at one pass.

What follows is a list of prepress, press and finishing equipment operating in an eastern book manufacturing plant. Note the variety and depth of computer-based equipment in the pre-press department. Plus three wide (40- and 50-inch) multi-color presses and three single-color perfectors which print on both sides of the sheet with one pass. The smaller, 25" by 36", press is most likely used to produce ganged covers.

The Best Printing Price

Equipment List

Capital City Press, Montpelier, VT 05601

Our equipment route can take digital or conventional analog tracks. For every piece of digital equipment there is an analog twin throughout the plant.

COMPOSITION:
Framemaker Composition.
    5 PowerMac 7100/80
    1 Quadra 800
Miles 33 Composition
    3 Sparc 5
    1 Sparc 1
    2 SunSparc SLC

File Conversions-Coding
    1 486 PC

Page & Galley Proofs
    2 QMS 1600 Printers

Scanning: Image Manipulation
    Crossfield C4000 4-Up
    Sparc 20 W/Adobe CPSI
    PowerMac 9500/132

Scanning: Color/B&W
    C6250 Color Scanner
    PowerMac 8100/100
    1875s Highlight Scanner
    486 SCO Unix

Proofing & Plating
    Linotronic 330
    RIP 50
    Xitron RIP
    UltraSetter 94e

    Sparc 20 w/Adobe CPSI
    Crossfield C8000 Drum

Offset Printing Presses
    6/Color 40" wide Speedmaster
    5/Color 40" wide Planeta
    1/Color 50" wide Planeta
    l/Color Mann Perfectors (3)
    2/Color Sordz 25" X 36"

Bindery
    Muller Saddle Stitchers
    4, 15 & 24 pocket

The Best Printing Price

Web presses, which print on rolls of paper instead of on sheets, are not usually economical for short runs. On the other hand, orders for 2,000 books and more could print on webs as long as the trim size of your book and signature requirements match capabilities of the equipment. These questions are best answered by the customer representative of the book manufacturing company with whom you're negotiating.

Also consider the specialist book manufactuers. One I know does only 6- by 9-inch books. That's the only size they do at a per-book cost lower than most other shops. They run only one make of small web press. From them you could save money and receive good quality, if a 6 by 9-inch book meets your requirements. Another company offers a number of sizes from a variety of web presses. Here a 5-3/8 by 8-7/16-inch book is less expensive than a 5-1/2 by 8-1/2. That is because several of their web presses print on narrow-width stock to lower signature costs from a press that provides on-line folding and runs faster than similar-size sheet-fed presses. In some instances web-press operators offer several different sizes of books at the same price. The primary question to ask your printer's customer service person is "How should I design my book to have it produced most economically in your plant?"

If there's a book manufacturer nearby it's definitely worth an educational drive to visit the plant. When the parking lot is full of employee junkers you're probably visiting a plant where the staff has little pride of ownership (read that one as pride in their work) and most employees were hired at the low end of the wage frame. If the reception area is cluttered and confusion reigns, so does the plant. A dirty press room with employees chatting while the press spits out printed paper indicates tradesmen with little interest in monitoring product quality, which could affect your book. The other side of the coin is a clean press room with pressmen watching output continually. What impression does the shipping dock and trash bin area make on you? A disaster area speaks of waste and more confusion. This situation translates into high prices for substandard work, or substandard work destined for insertion into the cartons of books they're likely to ship to you.

Somewhere in the heart of your visit will be a Customer Service person. The following report tells what they're all about, as abstracted from a major business magazine for printing management.

> *"The (State) Printing Sales Club presented its Lifetime Achievement award to Gary _____ for his extraordinary accomplishment of selling in excess of $10 million annually (in printing) for ten consecutive years. Not incidentally John _____, Gary's long-time boss, commented "Winning for Gary consisted of not only getting the order but getting it at the highest possible price."*

The Best Printing Price

Two points are obvious in this trade paper report.

The Customer Service rep (Gary) is not your best friend. Secondly, book production prices are negotiable.

There's additional reasons for going to all this multiple-bid trouble. Recently I had a small job for which final bids (RFQ's) were requested. The lowest was $1900 and the highest was $3950 for the identical short run book. And that's not unusual. Low bids may result when the factory's estimator misses a few critical specifications of your RFQ, substitutes a low-cost paper instead of what you ordered or the plant needs business so urgently they'll do your job at a break-even rate just to keep their employees busy. A higher than average bid could return from a printer who does not want a short-run book, has to buy too many services (negatives, folding or binding) outside, has estimated the job on the wrong size and type of press or adds big money just to deliver it to your front door in the company truck.

Let's move on and walk through a typical quote form which follows. As you will soon notice there is no specified delivery date for the books. It's a good idea to add an agreed upon date to your contract. Details of the sample's book bid specifications are on following pages so you may review them, as they might apply to your book.

The Best Printing Price

Typical Book Printer's Bid

RE: Your book.

We are pleased to submit specifications and prices.

QUANTITIES: 1000,
                add'l 1000's
TRIM SIZE: 8-1/2 x 11

TEXT: Copy - customer furnished layouts for one shot per page or book output to disk with Postscript per our specifications.
Press - via offset lithography, prints black ink throughout. Stock - 70# Sterling Satin, 524 ppi.
Proofs - complete bluelines.

COVER: Customer furnished color separations and finish layout for our camerawork. Provide laminated color proof for color match.
Press - via offset lithography; covers 1,4 & spine print four-color process with lay-flat gloss lamination; covers 2 & 3 print black.
Stock - 10 pt. C1S

BINDING: Adhesive paper cover.

PACKING: Bulk pack in single wall RSC cartons on pallets.

SHIPPING: FOB our plant dock, point of manufacturing. Postage and courier charges additional.

TERMS: 50% With order, 50% by certified check or wire transfer before shipment.

PRICES: 1000 $3147
    Add'l 1000's $1314

ADD FOR BLUELINES:
    .55/Page

Prices subject to change upon inspection of customer furnished material and evaluation of color requirements.

These prices will be honored for 60 days from the above date, subject to price increases for materials which may been initiated after our estimate.

                                S/S.

The Best Printing Price

When signed off, any bid form represents your contract for a desired number of books and an impressive printing bill you'll pay before they arrive. There's also a lot of fine print on the backside of similar paperwork from the printer which is well worth reading closely. Should a hassle develop the fine print may control what, if anything, could be done about the problem.

BOOK TRIM SIZE: The most common book sizes, and accordingly least expensive because they run on more-or-less standard presses using mill-production sheets of paper, are: 5-1/2 by 8-1/2, 6 by 9, 7 by 10 and 8-1/2 by 11 inches. However, any size book you want can be manufactured at extra cost. In this area indicate if any of the inside text pages are bleed pages. These are pages in which photographs or art work extends to and past the margin. This is an expensive touch most often found in art books or impressive brochures selling penny stock in long-lost underwater gold mines.

QUANTITIES: The number to print can range from few to thousands. The clinker is that it costs as much to make printing plates and "dress" a press with plates and ink for 10 books as it does for thousands. 500 Is a good minimum for a self-publishing project that hopes break even or make a little money. 1000 Books is better if you believe you can sell that many. I usually ask for bids on 1000 and additional thousands. By back-figuring I can estimate how much the printer is charging me to start the job which is a part of the first 1000 books. And how many dollars he wants for each thousand books from there on, which is basically overhead, press time, labor, ink/paper, binding, a reasonable profit and delivery.

PAGE COUNT Your choice, keeping in mind that bit about signatures. Fit your book to presses with signatures of 8, 16, 32 or even 64 pages and you'll be on the low-cost side. End up with a 67 page book and that's two 32-page signatures plus those very expensive additional three pages to be printed by themselves.

TEXT TO BE PROVIDED AS: You can offer the printer camera ready text and art work, printed on quality paper by your laser printer or a service bureau, which he will photograph with a litho camera or scan on a professional scanner to produce negatives in his plant. You could provide the complete book on a computer disk (CTP) from which he can produce the negatives, or use the disk-to-press (DTP) process to go directly to the press without making negatives. Be certain to make known to your bidders if there are halftones (screened prints) or illustrations (art) on the disks. Many printers offer typesetting service from your manuscript as an expensive option. With guidance from local litho services you can ship negatives to the printer which he can impose into signatures for his specific presses. This latter method may save you considerable dollars or it may not. Price both.

The Best Printing Price

INSIDE TEXT PRINTS: With what? Black ink usually, but you could go fancy and specify a color for which samples must be provided. Book costs may or may not increase by specifying color inside depending on the type press your printer plans using and time involved with cleaning it before and after running color ink.

TEXT STOCK: This is the bit about paper thickness (weight), such as 50 lb., 60 lb. etc. Plus specifying if you want a natural which is not truly white, recycled stock which is pocketbook unfriendly, a smooth surface, vellum or glossy finish, coated or uncoated, a low-cost printer-supplied stock you like or an expensive quality sheet he will have to buy outside to keep you happy. Specify exactly for this one!

NUMBER OF HALFTONES: Note precisely how many pieces of art or screened prints you have pasted onto on the camera ready copy. Or you can send pictures with the job. The printer will shoot the halftone negatives and place them in position on the page which costs slightly more.

COVER TO BE PROVIDED AS: Camera ready laser prints from which the printer makes the negatives? Or on a disk with CTP, POD or DTP instructions as above? A plate-ready film composite which your local litho house could produce for you, the "mechanical" you have constructed on the desk, or as a camera ready paste-up for the printer's use? All vary in cost.

The Best Printing Price

OUTSIDE COVER PRINTS: All black ink or with color? If color, is it a color photograph printed by the four-color process or "spot" PMS colors? Are you supplying separation negatives or is the printer? The reproduction of four-color photographs or art work is somewhat complicated and I strongly recommend allowing the printer to handle everything here. All you would do is supply the color photo(s) or art and mark on a drawing of the cover where it, and all the type, should go. 4/C Printing is expensive but with covers selling books color may be your best sales tool. Less expensive covers use PMS colors you can select from an industry standard chart which the printer's rep can display for you or as specified by samples you provide. PMS colors are applied from low cost spot-color negatives or overlays. These are known as "mechanicals" if an artist makes them or just "PMS negs" if the litho service does the job. And while you're at it, ask about fluorescent colors. Some of them are awesome.

INSIDE COVER PRINTS: All black or with color?. Usually the book's inside covers, which are the backside of the cover stock, print in black because all they do is sell the book or other titles from the same publisher. Or whatever else you'd like to include; such as your picture, a short upbeat autobiography, or something about other books you plan to publish in the future.

The Best Printing Price

COVER FINISH: Ultra violet (UV) coating may be applied to the outside covers on the same press that prints the cover. It is recommended as effective and is very low in cost or "free" with the job. It reduces shelf and handling damage in the bookseller's store as well as slows fading of colors exposed to light for a long period of time. There are gloss and matte film laminations which cost a bit extra and brighten or dull colors depending on which surface treatment you select. The printer's rep will have samples of this modest variety of cover treatments for your eyeball selection.

COVER STOCK: Most common is glossy coated stock which can be in the 8 pt., 10 pt. or 12 pt. weights (thickness). Inspect samples of them all. The basic weight difference is stiffness and cost. Fine quality stock is whiter, costs more and folds more smoothly. Low cost stock is the opposite in all areas.

BINDING: Books can be perfect bound which is glue binding as is *Self-Publishing Made Easy* . This performs well and is generic. Notch-binding is a form of perfect binding which saves a bit of paper and is worth asking about. Saddle-stitching means to staple the pages together, a procedure best limited to books of 64 pages or less. There's also sewn binding and hard covers for that impressive and costly image-package some self-publishers produce in search of market profitability. Here's one to watch. Smyth sewn books and those notch bound

The Best Printing Price

can have the same margins. However if you're using perfect binding, allow an extra 1/8th-inch width in the gutter margin area to feed the binding machine a small amount of extra paper. Ask your rep for additional instructions on this one. Mechanical binding, such as spiral wire or plastic combs, will add from 35 to 50 cents to the cost of each copy of your book. The price variation is based more on quantity than on the material used as hand labor is involved. The big question here is; does the printer do the binding in-house or send it out. In is usually less expensive than the out for which he will charge a handling fee.

PACKAGING: Ask for the books to be bulk-packed in standard cartons. If you want the books individually shrink-wrapped here's where you request it. You can also have them multi-packed with 2 or more books inside one shrink-wrap. Shrink-wrapping each book, or books in a bundle of 2, 4, 6 or 8, is a useful expense to maintain them in peak condition. Few publishers do it because booksellers don't like to shelve plastic wrapped books. It's a no-brainer to figure this one out. A book wrapped in plastic stops the bookstore browser from opening pages to determine if it should be bought. Take your pick. Have great books in fine condition that no one opens. Or books to be easily inspected and purchased by shoppers.

SHIPPING: Insert your zip code from which the book manufacturer can provide a very close

The Best Printing Price

estimate of shipping charges. Some very wise book manufacturers benefit their customers by passing on their lower-than-tariff discounted shipping rate. Others will charge you the full load. COD is an extra charge as is directing that your books be delivered to a residence.

METHOD OF PAYMENT: Half down, with the other half when you return the proofs and okay the job for production, is often requested by book manufacturers. Better is half down with balance payable after you have inspected and accepted a few press-run samples of the finished and bound product. They can ship several copies to you after the job is off the press. A few wise printers are now accepting credit cards for short runs. Ask!

OTHER THINGS: Request that all art, negatives and flats be returned to you with the job. Order a few hundred extra, trimmed-to-size, covers-only for promotional purposes. Ask to be given excess signatures for use as mailing inserts. Specify that overruns will be priced at the second thousand price, not the first thousand price. There's a big difference here because a printer has the reasonable right to run as much as 10% over your order. This means you're likely to receive, and be asked to pay for, 1100 books instead of the 1000 you ordered. This is a very fair trade custom as it is really difficult to start and stop a big press right on the dot. They just don't work that way. If the first 1000 was at the rate of $3.15 a book, and the second

The Best Printing Price

1000 was at the rate of $1.31 per book; at which rate would you rather pay for the extra books?

For a moment, let's take another look at the typical bid presented earlier in this chapter. Did you notice that under Press the bid form stated "Proofs-complete blue lines." Which for a fast reader could indicate that bluelines are included in pricing. Further on it is stated that bluelines are ".55/Page" which, for a 200-page book, would add $110 to the cost ! Under Shipping there is the note that "Postage and courier charges (are) additional." That means you will be billed for every letter and proof the printer ships to you. While the last paragraph tells you that the bid is not firm and, should prices of anything change, you'll be the one to come up with extra money. Great protection for the printer but not what most of us consider to be a "firm" price. My final note is that the foregoing "Typical Bid" is an actual price quote from a book manufacturer.

Somewhere on your agreement, in large letters give the printer the name and telephone number of the person they should contact with questions and from whom they can get immediate answers. This one will do much to keep your book speeding through the plant.

Now brace yourself. "Sticker shock" is next.

Evaluating Book Bids

When your Request(s) For Quotation (RFQ) return as a bids, you'll be in for "sticker shock." Keeping in mind that all book manufacturers were asked to price the same book in the same quantity, here's a few things you may find or should look for.

Substitution of a slightly smaller book than the size you requested. Specifying a "just as good" thinner paper, or paper of poor quality but not including a sample for your consideration. Not providing any samples of paper stock you specified or submitting a sample book they have printed which does not come close to your specifications. Pricing your cover run as a four-color process job (expensive) as compared to pricing based on the less expensive "four PMS colors" you specified. The first is the reproduction of a color photograph or piece of art. The second is color printing of a simplicity most easily found in a color cover which does not have a photographic reproduction on it. There's a place for either one on a self-published book but which one did you specify in your RFQ? The substitution of "notch" binding (less) for "perfect binding" (slightly more). Or stating that blueline proofs, if not included in the quotation, will only be provided at extra charge. Most book manufacturers include them as a part of the total bid price and will so state in their bid.

While reviewing bids also look carefully for the clinkers. Such as charges for shipping and handling their sample books or bluelines, adding postage, UPS charges or, as one printer tried to lay on me, telephone calls. The cure is easy. Just line the clinkers over with a big fat black marker on whatever bid approval contract you return to them. Separately adding such items to book production charges is double-billing that only a serious bean-counter would consider to be a good business practice to discourage repeat customers.

The bottom line is that RFQ price quotations should not be the sole determining factor as to where you do business. More important is what you are going to get for your money and an absence of smoke and magic charges which can escalate into big dollars for you to pay to obtain your books. The previous bid response is repeated on the next page.

Evaluating Book Bids

Typical Book Printer Bid

RE: Your book.

We are pleased to submit specifications and prices.

QUANTITIES: 1000
        add'l 1000's
TRIM SIZE: 8-1/2 x 11

TEXT: Copy - customer furnished layouts for one shot per page or book output to disk with Postscript per our specifications.
Press - via offset lithography, prints black in throughout. Stock - 70# Sterling Satin, 524 ppi.
Proofs - complete bluelines.

COVER: Customer furnished color separations and finish layout for our camerawork. Provide laminated color proof for color match.
Press - via offset lithography; covers 1,4 & spine print four-color process with Lay Flat gloss lamination; covers 2 & 3 print black.
Stock - 10 pt. C1S

BINDING: Adhesive paper cover.

PACKING: Bulk pack in single wall RSC cartons on pallets.

SHIPPING: FOB our plant dock, point of manufacturing. Postage and courier charges additional.

TERMS: 50% With order, 50% by certified check or wire transfer before shipment.

PRICES: 1000 $3147
    Add'l 1000's $1314

ADD FOR BLUELINES:
       .55/Page

Prices subject to change upon inspection of customer material and evaluation of color prep requirements. These prices will be honored for 60 days from the above date, subject to price increases for materials which may occur prior to final shipment of the completed order.
        S/S.

Evaluating Book Bids

Behind the scenes of an RFQ printers speak of "hit ratios" as a measurement of the ratio of quotations to orders. Some printers "hit" only six percent of the jobs they bid on. Others "hit" 75 percent. Many report from 30 to 35 percent as their "hit" ratio. Which at your end of the table, telephone or fax machine reads as "negotiate." There's nothing wrong with auctioning off your job to the printer you like best who's price meets competition.

Printing contracts allow for overruns and underruns by ten percent. You want a thousand books. The ordinary and common vagaries of paper cutting and press startup can eat a bit of stock which could result in your receiving a few less than the thousand. On the other hand, most book manufacturers take advantage of the ten percent over clause and will shoot for 1100 books to improve their cash flow. Be prepared to pay a bit more than you expected. The clinker here, which I have mentioned earlier, is how overrun books are priced. If the first 1000 books are $3.15 per book and the second 1000 is $1.31 per book the question becomes how much should you pay for those 100 extra copies. $3.15 Each or $1.31 each. Eager printers will charge you the $3.15 each for everything. Those who would prefer to retain their clients will price additional 1000s at the $1.31-each rate. You can note your decision as to what you are willing to pay on the signed order which accompanies your deposit check.

Evaluating Book Bids

The sales rep's success in selling, and enjoying their well-earned commission, is money out of your pocket. All good reason to think twice and ask more questions. Be slow to pick up the lunch check until you are certain their pricing is in the ballpark with other bids you received and you are comfortable, at the personal level, about doing business with the rep. And may I repeat, if pricing is within a few hundred dollars of the average of mid-range bids; select the vendor with whom you feel the most empathy. Such a decision makes self-publishing life much more satisfactory because you're doing business with people you like. In addition, they may like you and be of great help in making your self-publishing project a success. A good rep is there to obtain the best he can for his employer. That's a given. But that same person can guide and advise you as no one else can as to how to make the best use of equipment and paper in his shop. Or suggest means of designing your book for less expensive production and become a valuable business advisor for a single self-publishing project or as many more as you accomplish.

After collecting three or more bids on printing a book you can fairly well establish the price for which you plan to sell it. Depending on your cost of pre-production (Do it yourself vs. hiring outside specialists.) you have a fix on the total cost and the retail price to be set. From cost you can establish a retail price based on a profit ratio ranging from 1-5

Evaluating Book Bids

to 1-8. In simple terms a book that cost you $2.00 a copy based on a 1000 copy printing, could sell between $10 (1 to 5) and $16 (1 to 8) on the booksellers shelf. No, you're not going to make $8 on that $10 book. What happens is this. The distributor will want to buy it at 50 to 55 percent discount ($5 to $4.50) so it can be resold to the bookseller at a 40 percent discount ($6) and hopefully sold to the book buyer at a full $10. Your income per book, at the 5 to 1, ratio could be at the minimum of $4.50. At the 8 to 1 ratio you'll gross from $7.20 (55 percent discount to the distributor) to $8 (50 percent discount). Looks good so far.

Here's where the pedal meets the metal and you have to fudge a bit on setting the selling price of your book. What about competitive books? If they're all selling in the $10 area, but your book will cost $4 each, what to do? The minimum 50 cents gross from a $10 book that cost you $4 is less than worthwhile. You can always think about pricing yourself above the market, say at $12 each. That's an "Ouch." Is the book's size and content worth such a price increase? Would you pay that much ($12) for a competitive title that appealed to you? Then how about the 8 to 1 ratio. Here the book would retail for $32 which is a monstrous price to pay for anything but an extravagant coffee table monument: Most of all when compared to competitive books selling in the $10 area.

Evaluating Book Bids

Final thoughts on the subject of pricing. For years we've been using the 99-cent pricing technique on the basis that 99 cents had buyer appeal because it was less than the even dollar. So most everything has been 2.99, 10.99 or 19.99. Today's swing is to even-dollar pricing for items $10 or over on the grounds that even-dollar pricing hints of integrity as compared to the "bargain" impression of a 99-cent product. Your choice. However, no matter what you do, try to keep away from any of the odd numbers and set prices ending only in the numeral 5, 9 or 0. Subtle selling. But whatever works; the benefits are yours to enjoy and bank.

Decisions, decisions, decisions. Painful. But needful.

What's next ?

All the above underscores the importance of negotiating a fair printing contract. Every dollar saved there is profit for you or more competitive retail pricing of your book. Good questions answered best by again evaluating competitive books reviewed while doing the initial market research. If necessary ask yourself: "Why is my book coming in with such a high expense factor?"

Many self-publishers believe there's nothing wrong with breaking even on the first printing of a book. In short, they sample the market at low cost by pricing it with competitive titles. If the title is a winner, they revise the text a bit or add a few pages, change colors on the cover, label it "Revised Edition" and pay for a larger print run to lower the cost per each. This new edition is then retailed for a slightly higher price. For example: Printing 2000 books at a time could lower the $2 per copy cost of 1000 books to about $1.50 for each copy. Should you target the $9.95/$10 price range you have improved your gross income considerably. This simple success formula provides a firm measure of encouragement for doing a second printing. Need I say more about doing a wealth of "figuring" while negotiating book production costs with a printer and considering at which level to price your title on the bookseller's shelf. It's all money in, or out of, your pocket.

Let's become package specific about saving money while dealing with printers. The following suggestions are from Thompson-Shore,a major short-run book manufacturing concern. Please keep in mind that the broad fluctuation in pricing of paper and presswork may throw the percentages off a little. But the logic is definitely valid and should be given your most serious consideration while evaluating bids. What we're going to do now is consider a number of specific money-saving changes which could have a major impact on costs of a typical book design and specification package.

This test package is a 256-page 6- by 9-inch book, Smyth sewn, hardbound, with each copy shrink-wrapped. Changing the paper stock from its original specification of a 55# natural stock to a 60# white would save about five percent on the cost of paper. Change again to a 50# white stock and the saving is as much as 20 percent off the 60# paper price. Dropping to a 50# natural stock from the original 55# could save as much as ten percent of the paper cost. With paper usually being about half the cost of printing a book, it's easy to appreciate that paper selection and printer-to-you pricing is a critical factor. Your sales rep should be able to sample you with stocks we've mentioned in this paragraph.

To continue: Blueline page proofs were included in the original price of this typical book project and they do cost a bit of money. One short-cut would be to require bluelines of only the first signature. This proofs out pagination for the opening 8, 12 or 16 pages of your book and would save about $110.00. Totally abandon the blueline request and savings could amount to about $175.00. Significant money. All you need do is trust yourself that the book was in good order when you finaled the job and shipped it to the printer. However, if you're unsure of your skills by all means order bluelines. They are your last chance to catch errors of text, pagination, cover assembly and copy arrangement.

Bluelines are produced by the printer after he has made the litho negatives and imposed them into "flats" from which book and cover printing plates will be made. From those same flats they image prints on a rather ugly yellowish paper with type and art reproduced in sad blue. The sheets are folded like a book and provided for your inspection. Things to look for while inspecting bluelines include pages out of sequence or upside down, art work inserted in the wrong place and of course that elusive spelling error you did not catch during the final editing. All can be corrected by the printer who will properly charge an arm and a leg if you are the cause of the problem; and make corrections free if his staff erred. Bluelines show you how the cover will appear minus colors. There's also a product known as Matchprint which shows how color photographs will appear on the cover. It's costly but necessary to be sure that the very important cover is what you really want. There are no blue lines if you are using the CTP, POD or DTP technique because you proofed the book in your office when the disk was output through your laser printer.

Original specifications of the typical package we're discussing called for "A-Grade" cloth on the hard-bound covers. Such quality presents a fine appearance. If the subject does not justify an A-Grade presentation, per-book costs could be reduced around ten cents a copy by changing to a good quality paper-based hardbound cover material.

Smyth sewing, which involves clamping the book together and sewing it along the spine, is the best of all worlds for binding but it's expensive. Going to notch or perfect binding, in which signatures are glued together along the spine, could

Evaluating Book Bids

reduce each book's cost by about 20 cents per copy depending on the quantity you order. And you're right, a glued binding is not as sturdy as sewn binding nor as easy to open flat. But; is sewing too good and too expensive for your book's potential market? If less expensive binding is used the book may be sold for less or show greater profit for you the self-publisher.

It usually cost about a dime (1999) per copy to shrink-wrap books individually. If such special treatment will sell more book's it's worth the cost. Otherwise money in your bank account may be more valuable. Besides, when you did the early market research, how many shrink-wrapped books did you find on shelves displaying your competition or any other books you've bought or been given. Alternately, if books are shrinked in units of six or so, they will remain fresh until you unwrap them.

Ask your printer's rep' "Who gets the freight discount?" Does the printer charge you the higher published tariff freight rate and pocket the difference between the discounted rate paid the trucking company and the full rate for which they could bill you? If the book printer is nearby, a company truck could deliver your new merchandise at no charge.

UPS and FedEx charges for overnight shipping are high. Unless you're in a screaming hurry consider instructing the printer to ship proofs and samples by Second-Day air or by Ground service if they're going to charge you for this service. Most printers ship free. If they don't, it's your money they'll be spending. Expressing your options is good business judgment with no harm done by asking.

And what about CTP?

Perchance you have forgotten, this is "Computer to Press" in which you send a computer disk and the printer returns books. It's similar to DTP and POD.

By 1999 most major book-production printers had fairly well organized their prepress operation to handle both laser-printed camera-ready pages, and text copy from computer disks. At that time, some were not passing CTP savings from their lower production costs on to the customer. They had a good reason to retain the savings because CTP equipment is expensive. Recovering their investment is good business sense until they've paid for their CTP marvels and your book shows up. Ask if they are passing CTP savings on to you or charging the same for a run made from conventional camera-ready copy as they do from computer disks. You could gain a reduction of 20 to 25 cents per page cost in their pre-press charges by changing from camera-ready pages to CTP. Here's how this figures. With a 200-page book and a printer charging $4.00 a page for prepress, your cost of this portion of the job is $800.00. If CTP saves you 25 cents a page, your prepress costs drop to $750.00 which is a useful saving.

Evaluating Book Bids

The catch is that a CTP computer disk must be completely trouble-free at the press end. Your selected printer will provide detailed written instructions for you to follow in preparing disks for CTP. Follow the instructions precisely and save. Ignore the instructions and bleed money. Many shops will encourage you to send a sample chapter so they can audit the accuracy of your computer work. Which sample testing should cost nothing. All the preceding CTP guidance applies to DTP and POD production as well.

Printers live in a world where cost of operating a press is, more or less, rather stable. But paper prices rise and fall with phases of the moon or the need for TP in Zamboanga. In addition there's the effort of obtaining a specific paper you'd like to have. The printer has to find it, perhaps pay a broker's price to obtain enough stock for your book, then listen patiently to your complaints about the high price of printing. The best answer is to determine which stock the printer may have an excess of, and will sell below the bottom dollar. Then temper your desire for something more costly. As usual it's your decision, your dollars and your potential buyer.

Another production factor which affects book cost is time of the year. Book printers are traditionally busy as hungry bees during the second and third quarter of each year. Which makes the slower business periods of the first and fourth quarter a good time to drive a better bargain for your printing. But not all printers have the same busy-slow cycle. Ask each bidding company about their slow time and the possibility of a discounted price if you release your book to them during that period. It's your money. Hang onto all you can.

Self publishers seldom qualify for credit when ordering a print run. This supports the very good reasons why a book printer wants 50% of the estimate money up front when you send them a book to be printed. The logic is simple. Paper makes up about 50% of a book's cost. You're sending enough money to buy the paper. The printer can handle the rest of his costs in house and be comfortable waiting for the balance due on your order when the book is completed and ready to ship. Of course, if you can't make that final payment the printer keeps the books and initiates a collection action for the balance due plus interest and storage. Good financial planning at this juncture of the job means the production schedule may be met, you'll pay for the books when they're ready and be able to sell them when and where you planned.

Having finally decided who is going to print your book, the next step is sending the entire package off to the book printer. This is the next subject which involves a bit more than taping a carton, buying postage and package insurance.

Sending It For Printing

The last, last, last thing to do before sending your book and prepayment check to a book-production printer is to telephone or fax your printer's rep.

What you want is verification of the RFQ which may have carried a time limit. It's no fun to ship everything only to be told two weeks later that paper/ink/labor/beer prices have changed upward and your book will cost 50 percent more than you expected. It's a sucker punch often tossed at self-publishers. From a few printer's point of view it's a "clever" ploy. The theory being that most self-publishers only produce one book, are unlikely to become repeat customers so get all the money you can while the getting is good. Such a situation can really mess up your plans, not to speak of the trauma of pulling the project back and moving it to your second-choice printer. My recommendation, should you face this trap, is to hold firm and request rapid return of everything you sent if they elect not to meet the pricing and terms of their RFQ. More directly said: "Do it or get off."

Many houses will send you a confirmation statement to validate their bid price and repeat back to you the specifications on your order. These report sheets are worth checking carefully to be certain business communications are well and happy. In turn, such a confirmation eliminates sad surprises when the product or final invoice arrives at your address with a request for additional money.

This is also the time to double-check your book specifications for Trim Size. "True" is the dimension you requested. "Press Trim" could be slightly smaller. Again verify that they are contracting to provide you with the specified text stock and weight, color and opacity of the sample you approved. The same with the cover, which specification should include a notation as to UV coating or laminate (Gloss or Matte) finishing that you prefer. If they'll do it, and many plants will not, ask to have a few press run covers sent to you for inspection prior to binding the books. This gives you a chance to verify color accuracy and finishing before the books are bound. Did you specify the shipping method? Residential and or COD deliveries are more expensive than the most favorable basic truck freight tariff rate.

Does your printing order specify the number of trimmed extra covers that you would like to have? They're an inexpensive way to improve a news release with something colorful that shows your book at its best. Booksellers may use them for window displays and they cost very little when requested at the same time you order your book run.

Another item to verify in the printing order is a request that the printer carton-pack and give you all left-over "bindery sheets" which you can merge with your news releases. Bindery sheets are sections (signatures) of the book, folded down to size, which are excess. When a book is printed, in eight signatures for example, it's impossible to have all eight come off the press in the exact same quantity. Once they bind the available complete sets of eight signatures the balance of seven sets remain unused. The total number of completed books is equal to the fewest number of signatures. All other signatures are overage and you may be able to obtain them for the asking and payment of cartons and shipping along with your new book.

For goodness sake, make a copy of that final contract before you mail it off. Years ago I was stuck with a super bad job of printing 2000 maps for no better reason than I did not have a copy of the final agreement. The printer's rep and I finalized the contract in their office, made notes on their press-room copy and off I went. The job was a dog. When I called to complain, and referred to our in-office agreement, the rep said "We've lost the press-room copy and I can't find it anywhere." That's called being dumb: I was.

A major problem for the printer will be if you fail to send a complete package. This means everything; your deposit check, cover with art or mechanicals, all text ready to go and a signed complete agreement as to what they are supposed to do. Include detailed and accurate shipping instructions to insure that your books are on the way as soon as they are completed and packed. When you slip up in this detail the job has to be sidetracked while missing information is obtained. Your book is delayed. On the other hand, if everything is ready to go the printer moves it into production and ships ASAP. Can you ask for anything better?

From a business standpoint, identify your check with something like "Per contract Job #_____" so there's no question as to what you're making a payment on when you ship the job.

Turnaround time from a book manufacturer may range from a promise of ten days to the usual delivery time of 30 days. But, and this one's important, trade practices give the printer a lot of leeway on meeting deadlines. Books are traditionally late in reaching small publishers for good reason. Each printer has only so many presses and people. These twin factors place a ceiling on plant capacity. If a major customer, ordering 30 or 40 books a year, drops a book on the plant manager's desk, it is going to be printed before your book is produced. Delays can run up to three or four months which is tough but little can be done except use your telephone often. Keep on top of your book's production schedule and complain bitterly when it falls behind the sales department's promises. Printing salesmen or customer reps can often be of great help in keeping a book on schedule. Bend their ears as necessary.

What may seem to be frivolous advice is this. When you send your book, and a check for 50% of the cost, off to the printer the only thing left for you to do is relax. It's all out of your hands. There's little the self-publisher can do but hope everything will happen as promised. The best that can be done is maintain a telephone log detailing the date and time of every conversation with the printer's staff people and exactly what was said by who (whom?). Should serious problems arise, you could refer back to such statements while complaining to the company's Chief Executive Officer.

The sigh of relief from sending your book off to press is well taken. But relax not too much. Though the book is out of your hands, there's a ton of activity to be organized. Such subjects, in upcoming chapters, include activating marketing strategies, planning to sell it yourself, organizing

Sending It For Printing

publicity programs and looking forward to a pleasant incoming flow of self-publishing dollars.

Now write a short letter explaining your project to every potential Book Club. You'll find their addresses are on the Internet and in the library's corporate reference guides. Inquire if the book club would like to have an early review copy or an even earlier laser-printed set of the same camera-ready sheets you printed in the office.

Very Good Busy-Work

While your book is away at the press locate a source
of packaging materials, either folding cardboard or
padded envelopes, and take a sample book matching
your design to their offices for a best decision on how
to ship. Folding cardboard boxes cost the most and
add something to your postage bill while protecting
a book better than anything else. There's a neat
shipper called a "bookfold" or "vari-depth" carton
which is available in a wealth of sizes. They are
adjustable for depth to protect one to three or four
copies in the same order. Padded bags are lightest of
all and real postage savers. However they can be
hassled and occasionally result in bent or edged
books which are usually promptly returned.

Very Good Busy-Work

The key question here is that some packaging material will jump your postage costs to the next higher book-rate classification, in 1999 a 45-cent increase. More expensive protection may be lighter and reduce postage costs. The packaging supply company should have a postal scale somewhere in their office so you can test a variety of containers to decide on the best packing versus the lowest postage or UPS cost. Which suggests a telephone call to UPS and FedEx for their competitive shipping cost charts while you are considering USPS postage charges.

There's also a need for mailing labels. Ask the Post Office about the appropriate form of notice for shipping books at the lowest cost. Have that specific text printed somewhere on your labels to save postage while using the rate for books. Also obtain a current rate chart so you know precisely where book postage jumps to the next highest classification.

Now's a good time to review References in this book. Business resources and supportive materials you'll find include Federal Agencies, and trade and consumer associations. They're with *Self-Publishing Made Easy* as a good sampling of the vast wealth of material covering the field of book publishing. Those listed are valuable resources to make your self publishing more profitable. On the other hand additional addresses specific to the subject of your book will be found in the public library's reference section. While researching take a bit of time to look for trade publications who may do book reviews.

Very Good Busy-Work

Being practical is the name of the book game. Resources in the specific field of self-publishing change their name, location and existence with alarming regularity. Some are here today and elsewhere tomorrow. Accordingly I have listed resources of long standing and am directing you to other sites for current information from which you could abstract subject material.

There's a lot of writing and preparation to be done to obtain publicity breaks for your upcoming book. The best time to do prep work is now, while your book is being printed. It'll give you something productive to do and keep your mind off worrying about when the cartons will arrive. An additional area of effort is to firm up your marketing plan. What to do first and where. List all useful names, addresses and telephone numbers on paper so you can check them off as you proceed to mail or call. This is particularly important with news releases so you don't accidentally mail twice to the same media person which, as you can imagine, is sudden death.

I'm going to digress to mundane matters in early paragraphs of the next chapter, "Your Books Arrive," to smooth physical problems of storing hundreds of pounds of printed paper. After that's under control we'll charge into preparing to be busy with the many marketing and public relations programs which are essential to your self-publishing success.

Your Books Arrive

Suddenly, during this hiatus of the self-publishing event, you're going to be told that books are on their way and will be delivered soonly. They'll show up from an out-of-town printer in cartons, usually tied down with plastic wrapping onto a wooden pallet. A local printer ships loose the cartons in the company truck.

Where to put all those books?

Space in the family garage is ideal because dry storage is important. A thousand copies of a 200-page 6 by 9-inch book will need cubic space of about 4 by 4 by 4 feet. Or long narrow floor space along a wall two feet deep, four feet high and eight feet long. Build it yourself or have a friendly person make an open floor-grid platform of "two by four" timber on which the cartons of books can be stacked. Or pile them on your wooden trucking pallet. Either of these will keep your new inventory a few inches above the floor on the off chance the water heater might decide to drip all over the place. Also buy a waterproof plastic cover from the hardware store. Toss it over the stack for protection in the unlikely event the roof springs a leak during the worst rain of the century. Not only did the books cost you money, and represent a wealth of blood and sweat, but they really do sell better undamaged.

Cartons are marked with the title and number of copies therein. But trust not. Before you ship any unopened printer-packed cartons to a distributor, count the books. Not often, but enough to be bothersome, the book count will be off and you could be shipping more books than will be paid for. Or, on the other hand, be shorting the customer and receive a somewhat unfriendly telephone call. Such product count audits are common to all commercial transactions and do not represent an attempt to cheat you. It's just a fact of business life.

With books on hand you have the personal obligation to file your copyright notice with two books and a check for the filing fee. Also send a copy to the Library of Congress if you made an LC filing. Addresses are in the "References" section.

Those two are the important legal things. Now to preliminary selling efforts.

Your Books Arrive

Every distributor who handles books on subjects similar to yours will want to see a copy with a news release so they won't have to read the entire book to determine what it is all about. Same with jobbers and anyone else you can think of who could sell your product in quantity. Because these companies change their names, addresses and sometimes existence, I've provided only a basic list in the "References" section. You may locate others from fellow book publishers, Publishers Weekly magazine or industry reference guides in the public library under "Book Distributors."

A sample copy of your book, with its news release, should go to each local media office. For print it's mailed to "Editorial: Book Review Editor." For radio or TV send it to "Producer: Interview Shows." The area telephone book has addresses under Newspapers and Radio/TV headings.

On a national basis check the local library for the index they shelve which lists magazines published in the US. Send a sample copy with a news release to those publications with the most circulation and the most likely editorial interest in what you have produced. This is a lot of free books, a healthy postage bill and tons of work. But it's the old story. "If your light is under a bushel (basket) it does no good." Expose your book to every reasonable source that could enhance sales. Books for review are a low cost item to publishers and the most effective promotional package you can create. After all, you're seeking thousands of dollars worth of free advertising which makes book donations a most cost-effective trade-off for media exposure.

Mail promotional books at the lowest book rate. Special service or Express mailing really adds up to being expensive when you are sending out several dozen, or half a hundred, books. On the other hand, when a media person telephones to request a copy of your book for possible review; ship it overnight to arrive the following morning while the iron is hot.

Stuff a carton of the new books in your car's trunk. Not only will the car ride better but you'll always be prepared to sell a copy or two as the opportunity presents. Such a back-up supply will prove helpful to stock a newly-found bookseller who's ready to buy at that moment and may not be interested at all a week later. To support such guerrilla marketing you should carry a pad of generic invoices from the local stationary store.

Concurrently, telephone every bookseller within shouting distance and offer to do author signings, that is if you plan to do signings. Prepare a well-written, very brief, tele-marketing script to read when you call to present yourself at your very best. Booksellers usually schedule author appearances far ahead. By telephoning early you can set up a comfortable schedule and have time left over to care for the multitude of other programs connected with marketing your new book.

Your Books Arrive

Perhaps you could consider much of this chapter as "things to worry about" because you'll find that following pages bloom with greater detail on publicity, marketing, distributors and jobbers. Which makes this near-final stage of self-publishing worse than being involved in a wedding: All preparation and no action. But equally necessary. Read on and grin in anticipation of completion and reaping the rewards of a job well done. Your name will be on a book that readers are plunking down hard-earned dollars to enjoy. To reach them all you have to do is promote the dickens out of it, which I'm going to explain in the next chapter.

Local booksellers in your immediate area could be a wonderful help. Tell them again what you're doing, drop off a sample copy and check back in a few weeks to obtain their comments or orders. Often you will benefit from suggestions on slanting the marketing approach to specific groups or promoting it in a manner you had not considered. Even better, they may have decided the book is highly salable and order copies for special customers or shelving. The area public library system could want books contributed as coming from a local author or may bbuy copies for every branch in the County.

Marketing Your Books

Author signings in markets, book stores and malls are a mixed bag. In effect you and your book are a dog-and-pony show benefiting the sponsoring store or site while you hope to sell enough books to make it worthwhile. Consider it to be a reasonably good scenario when selling 20 books at one signing. The book sells for $10 and your gross is about half of that or $100. To earn this you had to pack books in your car, drive XX miles, get the books into the store, stand near a table for one to four hours while smiling brightly, talk with potential buyers, sign autographs, box left-over books, check out with the cash register and make your way home. Exhausting. If the money is worth the hours, it's a good deal.

However there's a very important plus to signings that is far more valuable than dollars. Book store managers talk to each other. If you are successful in one store, they are likely to stock your title and tell other managers about the book's merit. This inside-the-trade ruboff is important. Either way it's your decision as to how far to go. From my point of view one or two signings for each book I publish is extremely valuable. Not so much for the books sold, but as a means of gathering useful first-hand opinions about what I have produced. And, believe me, you can learn a lot by listening and watching pages turn under fingers of those who do not buy. Observe closely which pages they read, investigate casually or pass over. It's a low-cost education in book publishing and/or another book.

Marketing Your Books

Local clubs such as PTA, Rotary, Lions, etc. often welcome author/publishers as luncheon speakers. Take books and offer an autograph for those purchasing. From audience reaction to your presentation you can learn more of how to increase the success potential of your effort. The speech can be simply what you wrote about in your news release, expanded to fit the time. Use 3 by 5 recipe cards to carry notes and flail away with friendly gusto. It's a good feeling to speak to people you know who will buy the lunch and laugh with you often.

What we're really talking about here is a simple fact of self-publishing life. You and you alone have to market your book. This is only one of the many hats you're wearing: From creator, writer, editor, publisher, public relations practitioner, bookkeeper and general factorium, you are both the ballgame and the team. Profit from your book rises and falls on how well you sell the product every time you turn around. As simple as carrying that box of books in the trunk of your car. You really can't plan ahead to know when someone will buy one or more. Or a store appears on the horizon where the manager would shelve it for your/their benefit when you deliver on the spot.

Book shows are often a waste of time from my experience. There are so many books on display, usually with only the spine showing, that another book has all the force of a snowball in hell. On the other hand I know of several self-publishers who had the good fortune to make the right connections with major publishers at a book show. One local woman locked into a distributor who was looking for a title just like the one the self-publisher was carrying. It it was her first book. Needless to say, both publisher and distributor expanded their bank accounts from the title's success. However, the one-book self-publisher usually sells little or nothing at such shows. If you want to try, find a distributor who will display your book face out for a flat fee ranging from $50 to $150. Such a test provides an idea of how successful more of the same could be.

Somewhere along the line you'll bump into the idea of using a mailing list to broadcast wide the announcement of your book. Not a bad idea if the list is selective because such mailings are expensive. A horrible idea if the list is not selective and you're expending time and money on media or people with absolutely no interest in your title or subject.

Advertising is generally considered a waste of everything for a one-book publisher. There's just no way you can make an effective impression in the book trade. On the other hand advertising is the only cost-effective way you can sell a specialized book by mail order. Pick publications specific to your book's subject and go for it with small display ads or classifieds. If you get enough results to pay for the ad you're ahead of the game and you may wish to test again with more impressive space. If replies are totally absent, either the product (book) has no appeal to the publication's readers or your copy did not pull. Try a totally different ad which the publication's staff members might prepare to sell another bit of space.

An unusual final suggestion that has been somewhat practical is to advertise a book, in carefully selected niche publications, that is completed and ready but not yet printed. Or present it to local bookstore managements on the basis of a dummy cover. All this being done before you spend a penny on printing. No response. Negative attitudes. Don't print. On the other hand if you generate orders: The booksellers will wait. Mail orders can be held for 30 days or, best of all, explain to the client that there will be XX days delay in filling their order. Do they wish to wait, or should you return the money. Play fair on this one to keep out of trouble with the postal authorities. At best you'll sell some books. At worst you'll save a ton of money by not printing a book that demonstrates absolutely no sales or prestige potential.

Some books are sold in volume by inexpensive radio spot announcements at odd hours of the day or night. Cable television is a low-cost medium while broadcast TV is not worth considering unless you have a private money press.

In all of the above a prudent publisher places one toe carefully into the water but slightly, spending as little as possible to test the value of exposure. If it feels good and sells, then go for more.

If not, repeat advice in paragraphs above before worrying about what's in the next chapter. It explores the mind fields of marketing a new self-published book through jobbers and book distributors, aka. Big Warehouses Full of Books

Distributors, Jobbers And You

An important facet of self-publishing action is how one markets into both independent and chain book stores.

Certainly, you can solicit orders from small neighborhood shops, ship books, collect money and enjoy a maximum of incoming dollars from each sale. Such booksellers will want you to discount the cover price by 25% if they buy one book at a time using the STOP or SCOP order form accompanied by a check. More than two and they will ask for a 40%, or slightly greater, discount depending on how eager you appear. Their retail sale of a $10 book grosses you $7.50 (@ 25%) or $6 (@ 40%), from which you deduct all costs (shipping, production, printing, etc.) to come up with dollars per book for your time. Which, in such a simple selling, mode may be a high return for effort expended to move a small quantity of books the hard way. Next up are the really big boys: Nationwide book store chains, internet book retailers, warehouse discount stores, food market organizations, chain department stores and specialty shops where cross-selling takes place. To sell books in carton quantities into this market you must deal with a jobber or a distributor. There is considerable difference between them as to how they move books through trade channels.

The jobber maintains a traveling sales crew and a telephone, fax or e-Mail in-house order desk. In theory their business is selling your title to the major buyers. Jobber travelers are employed to display your book while telling store managers or retail buyers how great it is. Many of them do an excellent job and will move your book in ways you've never heard about. The few who don't, add fuel to the considerable argument about how grossly ineffective they are in proportion to cost of sales. Jobbers will ask for a 55% discount from the cover price plus a 10 to 15% percent commission on dollar volume of their sales. This is more than fair, considering effort involved. However such a commission structure lowers your income from the $10 book to about $3.98 a copy, based on a 55% discount plus 15% sales commission. It's one way to go, if you can afford a jobber for your self-published

Distributors, Jobbers And You

title. You may find them doing a rewarding job and sending impressive checks every month to brighten your mailbox.

The wholesaler, a different breed of cat, also wants a 55% discount off the cover price. They usually request that you consign a small quantity of books so they can stock the title without paying out any money until after the book is shipped to a bookseller. Their payment schedule can range from 60 to 120 days after the book is sent off. Why? Because it usually takes 30 to 60 days for the distributor to receive money from the bookseller from which income they will pay you. What is currently (1999) problematic is that a few major distributors have changed their policies and no longer handle a single self-published title. Nevertheless, no matter what you are told here or anywhere else, be sure to send a copy of your new book and a news release to every major wholesaler. For all any of us know, their "Title Selection" people may have been seeking a book on your subject or the company's policies have changed. Accordingly, if the package is suitable for bookstore distribution the wholesaler may stock the title without regard for it being self-published. Many distributors have catalog and marketing programs you could join to obtain additional exposure and sell into expanded market areas only they can access with efficiency

Distributors, Jobbers And You

To move books into the major markets you, in effect, are placing books you own onto a store's shelf in hopes someone will buy said books. And if you think that's rough, wait until you read about "Returns" in the next paragraph.

They're something else.

One small eastern distributor of books recently reported trashing over $30,000 worth of returned books. Why? Because a chain of book stores had sent them back for credit after reducing the level of stocking in all their stores. The original publishers had been paid but refused to accept the returned books from the distributor who had to bite that $30,000 bullet. Another wholesaler I know has a rack of such returns. They are sold as remainders at clearance prices so low you wouldn't believe it. This is where booksellers obtain stock to fill the "bargain" bin they usually stand by the front door.

Here's the how and why of "Returns". Usually major bookstore chains will only stock a new title from an unknown publisher on a "full return" basis. This means they buy the book and pay for it based on agreement that they may return it to the distributor anytime within a year for full credit. Sure, the book is supposed to come back in good salable condition. For a book shelved for eleven months to be in "good condition" is like believing in Santa Claus.

To encourage a distributor or jobber to distribute a new book, a self-publisher will be asked

Distributors, Jobbers And You

to to accept all such returns. In the ordinary course of business as the title is sold, the publisher will be paid. For books returned to the publisher anytime during the period the title was on the market the distributor wants those same dollars repaid. Be prepared when direct selling to independent bookstores to explain your personal return policy. It can be No Returns, Returns for Credit Only, Credit on Other Books (if you have others) or Returns within XX Months. This is an area of negotiation. So far no one has a clear solution to this mess which means one-title self-publishers are best off with a returns policy that somewhat matches the returns policies of area jobbers and distributors. It's a way of life in the book business. We all live with it though none of us really enjoy the added burden.

However, there's another and brighter side to this story. If you have no returns it demonstrates that retailers are selling all your books but not reordering new copies. Obviously, if they have no copies on the shelf no one can buy them. The best story here is to see that your books are on the shelf at all times and be willing to happily accept a few returns now and again. You may wish to offer the local booksellers a slightly better discount on purchases if they will keep your title in stock at all times for the eyeballs of every shopper in the store.

Chancy?

Distributors, Jobbers And You

It certainly is but that's the book business for large and small publishers. Many make a very good living so let's move on to your focused marketing plan(s) for success.

Marketing self-published books simply boils down to generating a demand for that specific book. This is a demand you're creating with every mailing and bit of publicity. Your hope is that the jobber, wholesaler, bookseller or store manager makes your book available.

With thousands of titles on the shelf, at any level of this distribution chain, there's no way any one organization can "sell" an individual title unless it's their mother-in-law's self-published cookbook or an equally monumental title. You, the publisher, have to generate every demand. About which I'll present a wealth of useful information in following chapters about print and airwaves publicity.

Meanwhile, closer to home, it's possible your book may be, best of all, marketed by speciality mail-order houses. A book on cooking could be sold through the mail by a firm who's success is built on the sale of kitchen hardware. They could picture your cookbook in their catalog then mail or fax resulting orders with instructions for you to ship directly to their customer under a "drop-shipment" formula. They'll want a 50% discount from the cover price and will reimburse you for the cost of shipping. Others in this field buy books outright (at a 50% or greater discount) and ship from their warehouse.

Distributors, Jobbers And You

Every time you see a mail-order catalog, that should display your book, is the right time to pitch them. With that suggestion on the table, we're going to move into the publicity area of selling books.

This involves an unusual mind-set which boils down to considering every possible opportunity to present your name, or title of your book, to the public. Then, once an opportunity is found, the next thing is to do something about it. Somewhat a reflex action closely related to shooting first and then asking permission.

In the long run, this is the publicity business and following chapters display it for self-publishers.

Publicity (Print)

There seems to be a ton of books written on how to obtain publicity for a self-published book. Please salt them liberally.

Such "How-to" publicity tomes often present the basic premise that if you do thus and so you will gain instant notoriety, sell jillions of books and bank a hat full of dollars.

Not so.

The basic guide with media is that guessing what works, won't. When a former President of Coca-Cola was asked about the impressive cost of their advertising and marketing programs, he replied; "I know for sure that half of our (advertising-marketing) money is well spent, and the other half is wasted. But we just don't know which half is which." This applies to publicity.

Publicity (Print)

Beneficial exposure, in the form of supportive book reviews or interviews, is free advertising in any form of media. Its appearance depends of one simple factor. That is: Will your book (or murder or winning a lottery) be of interest to the reader, listener or viewer.

A book about Aunt Emma may be wonderful to those who knew the great lady. Mine was a dandy. But her story is not likely to become a nationwide best seller. On the other hand a book which proves, beyond a shadow of a doubt, that the world is really flat could well generate a storm of critical comment and publicity throughout literate societies. Or land you in the funny farm.

So what to do? First reconsider the marketing decisions you made some chapters back after reviewing the competition. That's when you were deciding who would really want to read your book. Right now you're concerned with presenting a "why" they should buy it. Consider the following headlines which could be used on a news release. In it your are encouraging the editor to print the story about a new book or cause a reader to rush out and buy their very own copy.

AUNT EMMA'S STORY
GOVERNOR'S MISTRESS TELLS ALL
JOHN SMITH SAYS EARTH IS FLAT
SCIENTIST PROVES WORLD IS FLAT

Publicity (Print)

Is there any question about which of the preceding heads would cause someone to read the supporting material. Yet the first pair describes the same book. As does the second pair of hypothetical newspaper headlines which appear to ignore what holds the ocean in place.

Hopefully the message is clear. In writing a news release for any form of media, the headline (like that in a newspaper) is the key to obtaining attention of the person opening the mail. That person is very likely to be an intern or most recent hire; not the editor or decision maker. The headline should excite the letter opener while the body of your release must satisfy the editorial staff member who could approve a book review.

What else goes at the top? Simple stuff like NEWS RELEASE centered. Your publishing company's name, address, tele/fax number and e-Mail address justified to the right in single-line spacing. Plus the name and telephone number of an individual they could contact for additional information. Double space lines of the news release and limit the text to one letter-size sheet. One side of the paper only. If you absolutely must, use two sheets but never print on both sides of a single sheet. This is not a complicated affair but if you would like to learn more, there are many fine books in the library on the method of preparing such goodies. Or use the following format which has been abbreviated to fit on one page.

Coda Publications
P.O.Bin 711, San Marcos, CA 92079
Tel/Fax 760-744-3582
Contact: Joseph Rebholz
E-Mail to SDBooks@adnc.com

NEWS RELEASE

More than 1800 things to do, which are free or mostly so in San Diego County, are fully described in a new book by North County author Joseph Rebholz.

The 350-page book, *FREE THINGS AND MORE IN SAN DIEGO II,* has one complete section on scheduled no-cost or low-cost activities for families and individuals. The second section of *FREE* contains details and the location of hundreds of annual happenings such as civic festivals, exhibitions and entertainments open to the public.

The new book is available from regional bookstores at $16.95, or directly from Coda Publications, P.O. Bin 711, San Marcos, CA 92079. It is the latest addition to Coda's line of "Explore San Diego" titles, maps, computer games and videos.

-30-

Complimentary review copies are available.

Publicity (Print)

In the absence of such learning prepare the story (body of the news release) about your book and its availability in a simple newspaper-style report. The WWWWWH (Who, Why, What, When, Where and How) should be in the top paragraph. Sure, this is an old-fashion journalistic style but it is understood everywhere and carries the message in a useful manner. On the previous page was an abbreviated sample which may be expanded with additional information to fill the sheet with appropriate details about your new book.

Expansion of details in your release could report on how such an interesting or unusual book will benefit, entertain or educate the reader, listener or viewer. Tell more about you, the author, and list a city or state of residence. One paragraph prices the book and explains how the reader could obtain copies. For general releases that do not go with a book add a note below the end of your story, or hand-written stickie near the top, offering a review copy for a telephone call or e-Mail note.

Simplicity is the key to success of this initial step. Some media may print your material as-is if it is well written. Others will telephone or e-Mail for additional information and prepare their own story. Radio may telephone and interview you over the horn. TV may call and request your appearance in the studio. And, for sure, some uncaring editorial people may deem the material totally unacceptable and round file the release as not space-worthy.

Publicity (Print)

After you have considered the do-it-yourself method described above there is the usefulness of hiring a public relations representative. They cost money but can be highly effective. Often their personal address lists contain the names of specific media individuals who could/should be interested in your book. In many instances a good pubrel practitioner will telephone and literally sell your interview or appearance to the appropriate media person.

After you successfully achieve media attention at the local level, make copies of everything including newspaper pages and tape recordings of radio or TV interviews. Use the copies to solicit attention at the national level. This copy technique is a form of recommendation greatly appreciated by major media. From it they are given an opportunity to evaluate your interview qualifications. Accordingly, attaching a copy of the local newspaper article to the national media news release is often helpful. A note regarding availability of additional supportive material, as tapes or TV interviews, can be included with the offer of a complimentary copy of your book for reviewers.

As a dollars and cents thing, your book probably costs less than a news kit containing a release, photo and biography. I give books away at the drop of an interest. That is to media or anyone else who can support my selling additional books. It's not just one book I'm pushing but the entire concept of William Carroll publisher of a variety of books. It's all done under the premise that one hand washes the other as does one book sell another.

Interviews with media come off best when the author/publisher thinks in terms of entertainment instead of in terms of advertising. Give the interviewer and audience something to laugh about, wonder about and learn from. Your book then becomes a focal point to pique their impulse-buyer instincts. Proof of the pudding is in the number of movies you have attended because information presented by the coming-attraction "trailer" made the film seem interesting. The movie may have been a bomb but you didn't know that until after you had spent money for a ticket and squirmed through the show while suffering cold popcorn.

If there's any way you can tie your book into a timely or current topic...do so. One of my best publicity blitzes resulted from a practitioner tying *Superstitions: 10,000 You Really Need* into an upcoming Friday the 13th. Three radio and two TV stations provided interview time during a single day. We all had a ball talking about the good and bad luck of Friday the 13th while plugging availability of my book at frequent intervals.

Should the subject matter of your new book be ideal for libraries or other reference sources, promptly send review copies and a news releases to:

Library Journal, Book Review Editor, 249 West 17th Street, New York, New York 10011.

Publicity (Print)

Booklist, American Library Association, 50 East Huron Street, Chicago, Illinois 60611.

Publisher's Weekly, 249 West 17th Street, New York, New York 10011.

Kirkus Reviews, 200 Park Avenue South, New York, New York 10003-1543

The results of publicity efforts vary all over the calendar. Newspapers, radio and TV are usually almost instant hits or misses. From them you may feel results in a few days or a week at the most. Periodicals with a weekly or bi-weekly publication date can absorb as much as a month to give you any ink. Magazines, with long-lead times and monthly dating, could absorb up to a year before providing space to discuss your publication. The end run here is not to be impatient. Do your thing as well as possible and breath a sigh of "Thanks" for every bit of exposure. Just don't stop breathing. Continue to mail material to every newly identified media opportunity you can find. It's the continuing effort that pays off with print, as well as with radio/TV which is discussed in the following chapter.

Publicity (Radio/TV)

Radio talk shows are an author/publisher's dream. Not only will you be encouraged to speak about the subject of your book but you'll usually be allowed to tell listeners how and where to buy their very own copy through the mail or by telephoning toll-free to a 24-hour order desk you have arranged.

There are businesses that specialize in the promotion of talk show participants. Such promotions work well. One author reported 40 interviews in a short time, another claims to have sold over $100,000 worth of books while appearing on about 100 radio/TV interviews, a third author reported that one million of his books have been sold through radio interviews, and the co-author of *Chicken Soup for the Soul* has said that no one had heard of the book until he moved onto the radio talk-show circuit. Such promotion efforts could be well worth a try if you have a title that could generate mass-market interest across the nation.

And please note, I suggested talking about the subject of your book. This is the very best-ever way to encourage buying interest in what you have written and published, as compared to only talking about how great your book is. Arouse interest in the subject and soon the listener will get the message that your book has everything they'll ever want to know. Which is the basic reason most of us ever buy any new book.

Commercial advertisers pay serious money to pitch their product during station breaks. You, the author/publisher, get time to talk and helpful assistance from the interviewer for free. Free, that is, as long as your book appears to fit the news/information/education parameters of the media. In this instance, radio and TV.

When radio invites you to be interviewed, either in their studio or by telephone while you're in the home office, there's a few basic "needs to know" that will improve results of your presentation. Obtain the full name of your host-interviewer, a briefing on the station's audience objective (young, mature, rock, classic, etc.), approximate length of

Self Publishing Made Easy

time they plan for the interview and, most importantly, the host's usual format. Hosts range from kind to caustic, a string of hard questions, or kicking back and allowing you to carry the show more or less as you wish. Listening to the station's typical programming prior to your appearance date will answer most of these questions. If, for example, the host wants to talk about hunting and you pitch ecology, neither of you will be very happy and your air time will be short.

Additional simple things to know are: Date and time of the interview, the station's call letters, general geographic area they serve and name of the station's telephone receptionist. Why the receptionist? Because it is important that she (unlikely a he) be able to answer book inquiries a day or so after your interview. That's when a slow soul finally calls to learn how to buy a copy of your book. Provide the receptionist with a copy of the news release to be used as the source of information she'll need to help both the station and you. After all, she's the one callers will be sourcing information from. Be nice, it could pay handsomely.

If there's adequate lead time between the first appointment-making call and date of the media interview, advise booksellers in the station's service area about your coming show. Vendors will have time to lay in extra books and distributors will be happy as clams to benefit from your publicity efforts.

Self Publishing Made Easy

Publicity (Radio/TV)

Another touch is to forward news releases to the station's nearby newspapers announcing your radio/TV appearance schedule. It's a great help. Even more so for station-area booksellers if you mention their store name in the release. In the doing you gain useful publicity for the booksellers who could move an additional number of books. Newspaper readers often clip items of interest and act days later. As compared to Radio/TV which is a "do it now" publicity vehicle encouraging listeners to take instant action.

An owned or rented "800" number may be announced on air so that listeners can ring at no charge and place an order. There are telephone answering concerns that will rent you the use of their number, process credit-card orders at low cost and only charge a modest set-up and per-order handling charge. If not found, ask the nearest doctor's answering exchange as they'll be the one most likely to know of a local firm that does. Your book printer may offer similar services and ship the book for you or be able to recommend someone.

It's sales supportive to think "gifts" when announcing your ordering procedure and telephone number on the air. Consider the values of offering free shipping, a special discounted price to listeners, or no sales tax on orders telephoned promptly to your number. This form of special-offer support makes the station's listeners feel very special about

Self Publishing Made Easy

your presentation. To the point where they may telephone-order books while you're on-air.

Radio interviews are great fun so arrive at the station early to prepare yourself with a bit of free time ahead of your on-air appearance. You can relax to clarify your thoughts, rehearse possible responses and prepare to present yourself as competent and trustworthy. Carry copies of a 10 or 15 question and answer list to help the interviewer sound very knowledgeable and make it easier for you to come on as a very sharp person with fast answers.

When you're finally on the air the opening comment is best if warm and thoughtful with expressions of interest and appreciation for your host's efforts on your behalf. If possible, listen to the interviewer talk with someone else the day before so you will have an understanding of their style and demeanor. Try not to quibble. If you are evasive, you will be heard and/or viewed as not believable.

In the studio, or while doing a radio interview from your office or home telephone, it's the same ball of wax. As much as possible plan to talk about the subject of the book. Talking of contents and theme will make the most interesting presentation. In addition, listeners can become buyers if vocal enthusiasm hot-wires them with your emotion-creating tales about the book's subject. Once enthused, audiences "listen up" for purchase instructions you have typed for the interviewer to

Publicity (Radio/TV)

read to be certain there are no mistakes about addresses or suggested ordering procedures.

If by telephone, you can be comfortable in your home or office with a copy of the book handy. Stand up during the interview to make yourself sound better using full lungs not scrunched from a sitting position. You can expect to be asked often about your favorite, most interesting or the most controversial section of the book. Try to outguess the questions and use stickies as projecting index tabs so you can find appropriate pages in a hurry. Fast questions are best responded to in modest 15 to 30 second detail. "Yes" or No" is not what the interviewer is looking for. Entertainment is the name of the media game which may include your telling about why the book was written, fun stuff about completing the manuscript (On the kitchen table while tending beer mash.) or suchlikes to liven the interview. Pre-write an easy-to-read explanation as to where and how the listener can obtain a copy of your book. This makes certain the correct information will be passed on to the audience as briefly as possible. Best of all fun is participating during "call-in" interviews. You will be talking with listeners who can, and often do, ask the most outrageous questions. Meanwhile the interviewer, who is not likely to have read your book in detail, could be hurriedly fanning pages looking for his or her next provocative question. Should a question stop you cold, my best advice is not to panic. Soften the blow by making a somewhat related new-area comment or noncommittal response. It's all a conversation in which you are hoping to maintain a desired upbeat trend to the presentation.

While responding to questions, now and then seek the interviewer's agreement or acceptance with an occasional "Can you agree with that?" This gives you an opportunity to continue leading the interview with references to the last question discussed and/or a conversation shift into a new area.

It's great to be highly opinionated about your book's subject. Such an affirmative position creates strong audience reaction from those who agree and support you, and from those who believe you are all wrong and deserve their most vocal complaint. Both camps will buy books if they have been aroused to interest by your presentation. One side to join you and the other side to further nurture their dislike for your opinions or write contentious letters.

Interview over and home in the easy chair, please take time to promptly send a sincere thank-you letter to your interviewer/host and any other station people you may have worked with. Plus adding a line to your standard news release listing this most recent publicity to assure new media contacts that you are a worthwhile and interesting interview subject.

Publicity (Radio/TV)

Television interviews amid their theatrical settings are noted for being nervousville. That's because body language is so important in reinforcing your statements with positive gestures. Dress down to impress and smile a lot. Strange studios, hot lights, a microphone stuffed into or partially hidden on your clothing, people peering from behind cameras, sometimes a make-up artist patting goop on your face, an interviewer who has time to read only a few hurried notes about special questions to ask and suddenly you're on. Both of you should have books in hand. Smile at the interviewer and sit relaxed. If you do nothing else...smile at the interviewer and sit relaxed as they lead off with their points of view.

Think of all this as a conversation with someone you like. Be happy, funny, tell it like it is and continue emphasizing the values of the subject of your book. If you want the interviewer to take a specific action or follow your direction (Such as "Open my book to page 22."), speak clearly so there are no moments of confusion which could make the host appear clumsy. On the other hand, listen up for the interviewer's instructions or requests to you. Should a question be so detailed as to require what might be considered a confusing answer, break your response into sections and explain why.

A goof is a goof. Say something wrong or stumble, which most everyone can do, then quickly

Self Publishing Made Easy

231

make a clarification and continue as though nothing wrong had taken place. Near the conclusion you, or your host, will have time to tell viewers how to obtain your book. Here's a reminder; type this information on a small card and give it to the host so they won't err and mess up specifics of the ordering information. Many TV stations will be glad to dupe a copy of the show if you hand a blank VHS tape to the producer who brings you onto the set. Interface pleasantly with every member of the crew and offer gift books as a gesture of thanks for their help. They could suggest that a non-competitive sister-station or radio affiliate also interview you.

Sell Them Yourself

Often ignored amid the pleasures and problems of marketing books through trade channels and the media are the many peripheral sources of additional dollars.

Here are a few of them.

Selling subsidiary rights to your books can often result in nice bits of extra income. Letters to similar-subject book and magazine publishers around the world could offer to sell reprint rights to all or part of your book. Why magazines? Because in other-nation markets many magazines are produced by book publishers, or vice versa. Less obvious is to obtain mailing-list information by reviewing the local library's reference guide, *Books In Print,* to determine which overseas publishers have produced books with content similar to yours. Write all the logicals and if they're interested in releasing a special USA or foreign language edition they'll reply and ask for a review copy. Other reference guides to inspect are *Standard Rate and Data* and *Ulrichs Standard Periodical Directory* which are great sources of useful publication addresses. Go deep with these as the amount of information is astounding.

Military exchanges sell an enormous number of books as do a few other government agencies. Telephone calls to the nearest exchange or agency would be a good beginning to learning about acquisition procedures which vary widely from agency to agency. A few major corporations provide book services to their employees. I'm told it's is a real hassle to find those concerns which are active in this employee-relations field and even more of a hassle to find the precise person to contact inside corporate castle walls. So far the best idea that's been presented is to send a form letter and/or ask everyone you know if their company maintains an employee-only book store or will special order books as required.

Catalog merchandisers are a fine source of book sales as long as your subject matter is something they like and will help sell additional merchandise to their specific customer profile.

Sell Them Yourself

When you find a catalog that appears logical, write promptly and offer a sample copy for their consideration. In addition there are "premium" suppliers who could market your book in quantity for use as a give-away or self-liquidating promotional item. Banks are known to be responsive to giving away regional interest books they could buy from you, food providers like cook books supporting their specialty and automobile parts stores are strong buyers of books detailing auto repair techniques. When they buy in bulk you can expect a request for a discount. From 25 to 100, consider 20%. Up to 500, 40%, with a discount of 50% or more when they get into the multi-thousands. If they order before you print the title, their additional copies will help lower the per book cost because of the larger print order. Share such cost-saving benefits with bulk buyers while increasing your profit per book sold through the usual book trade channels. Catalog and premium houses are grouped among corporate listings found in the public library's reference book section.

Because I seldom watch television, you'll have to do your own homework on this one. Cable shopping channels, such as QVC Network, Home Shopping Net and ValuVision often pitch books. One woman reports selling more than a million copies of her books about healthy quick cooking. When you contact any of the shopping channels ask for a copy of their "Vendor Relations Kit" which will brief you on how to convince them effectively. It's said that books selling for more than $15 and less than $30 do well. If you have several books at a lesser price you could consider bundling one of each and selling the shrink-wrapped group for a favorable rate of return on investment.

And how about a few simple things. Print colorful bookmarks pitching your title(s) and give them away every time you appear anywhere. Your bookmark could list an 800 number for incoming orders or fax-on-demand for those who would like to sample a chapter or two. Should you have a web site? Not from my point of view. It's an internet jungle, costs money and is dominated by major operators and big budgets. Do you have a speciality that could be repackaged as a consultant service? And why not? Charge a modest fee to provide guidance helping someone else and sell them a book at the same time. Would your speciality support a newsletter? Turning your book into a video may be possible, and then again not. But it's certainly worth thinking about. A friend turned her book into a game but it didn't sell. Perhaps your's would. There's also personal note sheets, small calendars and rubber stamps. The latter being great to support a child's book. With the best advice I offer being "If you think of it, give the project a low-dollar try. The benefits may surprise you."

A good, one-page, promotional write-up and order blank for your book can be supportive in many

ways. Use a local copy shop to reproduce the cover of
your book as a portion of the order form you give
away at the drop of a hint. Letter-size copies are low
in cost and color paper adds a touch of class to the
impression. Copy any order blank you can get your
hands on, paste an extra cover in place and away
you go. With every book you sell out of the car trunk
or by mail, should go the same order blank and a
bookmark to encourage reorders for additional
copies. But not in copies for booksellers. They feel
poorly about a publisher being a competitor. The
same write-up may be recycled if the order form at
the bottom were replaced with a photograph and
short biographical sketch of the author. This latter
piece could be mailed to media not wholly related to
your subject matter with a handwritten stickie at
the top offering a review copy. And mailed without
the stickie to every bookseller you can think of as a
gentle reminder about earlier announcements of
your new book.

If your area has a convention center, and
hosts out of town visitors in bulk, you may have a
dandy market for corporate sales. These involve
selling your book to the corporation holding a
convention in your area then delivering books to
their host hotel. You could offer to provide a neutral
or overlay cover displaying corporate-supplied
information. Such books are used as "pillow gifts."
The corporation's welcome letter to its people is
inserted into the book which is in each guest's room

on arrival. It's a market and a good one. Local destination management firms, or the marketing departments of your major hotels, could purchase books to be given as gifts for their VIP guests.

Ask.

Now's the time for renewing your personal contact with local book stores and the Community Relations coordinator of metropolitan and chain book stores who are the people organizing author signings. After arranging for an appearance ask for guidance as to what you can do to help. They may find a use for flyers as shopping bag inserts, signs for posting in the store, extra book covers for window decoration or whatever. The coordinator may be able to provide samples of supporting material they like best. Also send the coordinator a few extra press releases and author biographies to enhance your planned appearance. They may have a friendly staff contact at local media who will use a press release related to your appearance in a specific store. This could happen though the same media didn't run your original "new book" announcement.

In the nuts and bolts department, find out how the bookseller wishes to arrange for extra copies that should be stocked for your store signing. Do they plan to place a special order with the distributor or prefer that you bring additional books with you? Should you be asked to show up with extra books, its a very good idea to have an employee check your stock so there is no confusion

Sell Them Yourself

as to whose books (your's or the store's) were sold during your author and book-signing appearance.

When you sell about five books an hour that's reasonable. Sell 15 an hour and you're very good. Anything over that is spectacular. And keep in mind that if you're a success, one bookstore manager tells another to keep you busy as long as the title moves.

Here's a few hints to make your book-signing appearances more effective. Have a local copy shop enlarge your book's cover to poster size in full color. Mount it on something that won't bend and hang from the front of your display table or on the wall behind you. If the store has a public address system, write a short announcement and give it to the manager for use as often as possible. Has any local personage endorsed your book? Make a modest poster from a copy of their note and place it where shoppers can read the message. If the manager has a media list, take time to call them all yourself. Request an interview and keep your fingers crossed that a reporter or radio/TV team will show up and make it a real occasion. As a side-note. Determine if there are concurrent local events near the proximate time of your book signing. Event sponsors may be open to your making a short presentation about the subject of your book, with references to the signing time and location.

Local newspapers usually carry notices of fund-raising events. When your book is relative to the event's theme, a door is open for the sponsor to

sell your books in return for a portion of the sales
price. By offering to consign stock you will make the
proposal most appealing to fund-raisers. The same
approach works with affinity groups and business
associations holding seminars or conventions in your
area. A self-published book on local history matches
objectives of the local historical society or regional
museum. They're a logical place from which to
market any regional title. Does your book's subject
matter lend itself to presentations you could make to
social groups and clubs? In the doing give everyone
bookmarks and sell freshly autographed books.

If on sale during your presentations, a big
book is better, color is even better yet and the
cost/profit structure is heavily in your favor. When
you have time, attend one of the free get-rich
"motivation" seminars where they sell three-ring
binders full of copy machine output with a blistering
color print stuffed under clear plastic on the front
cover for hundreds of dollars. The motivation people
make those of us in the book business look like
pikers. It is a good place to listen and learn while
your charge card was left at home.

Then to the lean side. How about packaging
one chapter inside a simple cover, with your
autograph and an order blank for the complete book.
Sell the one-chapter sample at seminars for a dollar
or two? Extra money for you from those who can't go
the whole route, with the potential of future mail
orders after they've become enthused.

Sell Them Yourself

There's also spin-offs. How would your book sell as an audio tape? Or book and tape in the same package? As a computer disk? A CD? Over $2 Billion in books on tape were sold in 1994 and more are being sold right now. One Texas audio-tape store, that handles nothing else, reported grossing $700,000 during one year. The nice part being that an audio-book seems to have no destructive affect on sales of print-on-paper products.

CD-Roms are another story. Ninety percent of new titles are reported to lose money and about half are never stocked by retail stores. The return rate is fierce and you'll find them discounted in factory malls to a ridiculous price. However the cost to produce is modest. About $5000 for the "master" from which duplicates can be produced for $1 or less depending on the quantity. But CD-Roms continue to sell, like over 50 million annually a few years ago. Check your local retailers on this one before you venture.

Do you want to try mail order?

Many reasons why not. Mail-order advertising is enormously expensive and the greater a publication's circulation the greater the expense. So let's come down to earth. A publication that editorially relates to the subject matter of your book has readers who also directly relate to your book's subject matter. They are definitely potential buyers and circulation numbers have little to do with it. On the flip side, major circulation to a general audience seldom pays off for the self-publisher. Hint: If a publication runs your press release or reviews the book, with resulting sales, modest advertising in the same publication may pay off handsomely.

A small advertisement with carefully written copy (See an L.L.Bean or Lands' End catalog for great descriptions.) can be an excellent test of your marketing idea. Selling copy works best when it quickly and clearly tells the reader two things. The first is how the book's subject matter benefits the reader of the advertisement. Secondly how they obtain a copy of your fine book. And that's it. Keep it simple. If it works, repeat. If not, try another publication. Nor is there a law which stops you from trying two or three publications at the same time. "Key" each ad separately with a tiny alteration in the address or name in the advertisement. Orders addressed to James Smith, Jay Smith and J. Smith could easily tell you from which print advertisement the order came. Another easy way to track the sale's source is coding your address. Such as PO Bin 711-A for one magazine and PO Bin 711-B for another.

If you can think of it, test minus big dollars.

Not one of the most difficult things about mail order selling, but the most difficult, is writing advertising text (copy) for your ad. Specialists exist who will do it for a price. Or you can learn and do a pretty good job because you know your product (book) better than anyone else. It all begins with a clear understanding of the reader/listener/viewer

you are addressing. Everyone has been pitched to
buy books. However when you know your audience
well the chances of success are multiplied manyfold.
Address lists for a broad mailing are available
easily. Some provide great response, some don't.
Most such lists contain about 25 percent dead
addresses within a year. If you mail to a niche list
(Doctors, Mechanics, etc.) you'll need to design the
envelope so your mailing will be separated from
other commercial mail and opened.

Somewhere along the line you have been, or
will be, involved in writing promotional copy to be
mailed to potential buyers in the form of a letter or
brochure. Here's where your best writing skills
should shine. Everyone can tell you what to do. I'm
not. Instead I'm including, right here, some of the
world's best mail-order copy from Martin Edelston's
Bottom Line Publications in Iowa. Mr. Edelston has
won dozen's of awards for his mail order programs.
Here's why. "These secrets save you big, big
money...How hospitals pad your bill...Age defying
secrets....Burn 1400 calories a week by drinking ice
water...How to trouble-shoot your own health." I'll
wager that you, like me, found these headlines so
effective that you would like to know more about one
or more of the subjects he's written about. Give
Edelston's approach considerable thought and plan
to do as well.

Being clever is not at all bad in mail order.
Recall all the "official" envelopes you've opened, the

oversize or colorful mailings, those awarding a huge prize, and the many others. A friend sent her publication announcement in a paper bag with a large heading near the address reading "Let Your B&B Out of The Bag." It went to all the B&Bs in her state. To brighten the brown kraft bag she used big and colorful commemorative postage stamps. The total response was outstanding. Often a mail-order pitch will contain notes on stickies, hand-writing on the side of a printed letter, or similar personal touches. And why not. What you want is attention and results. It could even prove worthwhile to insert copies of a number of brief book-reviewer comments from media, or your friends, with the promotional mailings.

Free things pull. You can donate free postage, a copy of your memoirs, rare stamps or almost anything of perceived value to those who order one or more copies of your book. A small discount for multiple orders is not a bad idea either. All of which offers are even more effective if your mail order letter enclosure is written on a one to one basis. Make it personal, light, pleasant to read and ask for the order in the last paragraph.

With the average rate of return from a mail-order solicitation being about two percent, anything you do to increase the numbers is worth considering. How about including a toll-free telephone number, your eMail address or web site URL. The easier it is for the order to be sent, the more likely it will be. Seasonal holiday mailings are said to be the best, but I question that for a single book. You're competing with too many very expensive gift catalogs and brochures. Somehow it seems that tying a title into a season (Travel in the summer, painting in May, sewing in January) would make more sense. Small test mailings for your specific title may be the better way to learn the answer to this one.

Somewhere along the line someone is going to suggest that selling books over the internet will make you wealthy. They'll point to several major sites that are selling thousands of books daily then sit back with big smile to await your blessing. The truth is sad. As of 1999 there were no known major internet book sites that were showing a net profit. Yes, some were marketing millions of dollars worth of books while losing money on every one they sold. They were not alone in being among the losers. An association of professional photographers surveyed their members. Most every member had a web site. No association photographer could report any business from the effort. Magazines have web sites and decline to disclose how many subscriptions they have received. Independent bookstores report no rush of business. A major bank put up a huge internet shopping mall and in eight months processed less than a dozen orders. It seems to be millions of "lookie loos" and few buyers. I suggest you not open a bank account on this one.

Money In The Bank

Self-publishing to make money is simple. Write
book. Publish book. Talk book. Take money. Deliver
book. Smile all the way to the bank.

Opening a bank account for your book sales is
a no-brainer but there's one thing to do that makes
life much easier. It hinges around the point that
when customers write checks for a mail order item
they're likely to make their check out to the author,
publisher, name of the book or Post Office address.
A few banks flinch at the deposit of checks bearing
any name but the specific name of your account.
Accordingly you may be requested to double endorse
the check; once with the name written on the front

of the check (Author, Book, Publisher, Address, etc.) and then endorse it again with the name of your account. The easy way around this is to buy a self-inking endorsement stamp which imprints your account name, account number and the statement "Prior Endorsement Guaranteed." This tells the bank that you guarantee validity of the check without regard for what the book buyer wrote on the front. Once in a while a customer will forget to sign their check. The same technique applies but you must write this one. In the top-most endorsement area on the back of the check write "Lack of Signature Guaranteed by (Your name)." Then place your endorsement stamp below your notation. Most banks will accept this form of check deposit if they know your account is in reasonably good shape. Ask on this one if there's doubt regarding your bank's policies.

Personal checks in the mail are neat and it's my experience that they seldom bounce. Request that other-nation buyers send their checks or money orders "Payable in US Funds" and you'll collect the proper number of dollars and cents without the trouble and losses of foreign exchange conversion.

Most mail-order concerns accept charge cards which is a plus for any self-publisher who plans to handle a number of retail sales. Your bank can advise you on setting up an account for which they may, or may not, charge a set-up fee. There are also services which will process your card charges and deduct their modest fee from the amount of money they remit to you. Shop around on this one as cost of the charge-card account can range from a fat money fee to a simple flat rate. Much of this is negotiable and your peers, or a mail order business in your immediate area, may well have excellent recommendations.

Meanwhile, the best of all financial planning includes arranging to set aside a bit of change, and original material, disks or negatives/flats on hand, for a fast reprint when you sell the first edition more quickly than expected.

We're now returning to square one of the book business. Distributors are big warehouses full of books. Booksellers are small warehouses full of books. Neither of them sell books. They just have books. For as long as you have inventory in the garage it will be necessary to continually publicize, promote and market your book in every way possible. When the public requests a book, the bookseller will shelve it. When booksellers order titles, the distributor may stock it and the inventory in your garage becomes smaller and smaller.

It all hinges on public awareness. Call it publicity or whatever. And it's all up to you, the author/publisher.

Some writers have made a ton of money producing and selling one or more books which means the door is open for another profitable venture into self-publishing.

Will You Become Rich

It's not likely. But it is possible.

A well-done self-published book of regional or local interest could go on selling for years. Regional or local interest books are those about local attractions, history or important events; such as the Johnstown flood. Similar books pay for the effort and show a modest profit while generating a long-term glow of satisfaction and income for the author-publisher.

The same applies to a book of national interest that has long-term appeal. Self-help, diet, cooking, business management and similar subjects have projected many a one-book self-publisher into the mainstream of multiple book publishing. Or they moved into the lecture and seminar circuit with additional self-published spin-off titles amplifying and clarifying the original work. You may even find some of these in book stores where the original work will be shelved adjacent to follow-up titles on the well-known premise that one book sells another.

A run-of-the mill title of general (non-specific) interest will have a tough time in bookstores because there are more than a thousand books published every week. A tiny percentage are blockbusters and make money faster than the government. A modest percentage break even or show a satisfactory profit. But many general interest trade books are money losers. If you consider this to be a questionable comment inspect "bargain tables" of major book retailers in your area. On sale, for peanuts, you will find impressive books which bear astronomical original prices. They're great as holiday gifts for people you really don't like and equally great as an object lesson about losing money in the highly competitive publishing business.

Chain book stores do it by the numbers. The buyer pulls up sales information on the computer monitor for every title the chain stocks. If a title pays for its shelf space and turns a profit within 90 days, the buyer will keep it in stock for another 90-day cycle. If not it is returned to the distributor and eventually to you, the publisher, for credit to be used to stock other and newer books or refund of monies paid. This is why it is so difficult to find a popular title you heard about six months ago but is no longer on the shelf. Clerks will special order a copy and you will receive it quickly if there are any left in the warehouse. In other instances, what was popular six months ago may only be available from the publisher or is out of print. Exceptions are regional or local-interest books which usually continue to be stocked as long as there is enough buyer action to justify their space on the shelf.

Self-publishing at its worst is a gamble. You have a superior concept this year for a book, to which pleasant conception must be added the effort of writing and production. A three-year cycle is about average. Do you know anyone who can determine, with certainty, what type of a book will sell well 36-months from date of "this great idea?" Despite such terrible odds, there are successes in the book field and self-publishers enjoy more than a fair share of them.

The reason for "more than a fair share" is that self-publishers, small-press and independent publishers are in the driver's seat in the book business. We know how to communicate and are willing to do it. We're not computer experts producing useless manuals telling us that desired information is in the same computer which has crashed. Or artists creating coffee-table books with more "wow" than wisdom. It's self-publishers who can observe and accept new ideas, then move forward without a meeting of the board of directors. Independent operations produce books as fast and usually faster than large publishers. We'll often be successful risking on the very subjects that large publishers would ignore because the observed potential market is too small for their corporate size. And in the doing self-publishers help readers learn, or laugh, better than anyone else.

It's the most exciting business I can imagine and with about 50 years of publishing behind me, I continue to look forward to producing more books and enjoying vacations often.

If *Self-Publishing Made Easy* seems like something you should do, give it a modest try. Your book could be one of the best sellers of our coming year.

The best of good luck to you.

Glossary

Application Program: Software used to create and modify documents. Some common types of applications are word processors, databases, graphics programs, page make-up software and communications programs.

Application Files: Files that are created from a computer program or software.

Aqueous Coating: A water-based environmentaly friendly coating for printed covers.

Back-Up: To save copies of files for safekeeping.

Glossary

Bernoulli Disk: An early type of disk used to archive and protect quantities of information.

Bit-Mapped Font: A computer type font of dots designed primarily for use on dot-matrix printers.

Bleed: When an image or background extends beyond edges of the final page or cover trim.

Blockouts: Rubylith window in black or red, a clean-cut edged area on disk and/or camera ready copy, used to place halftones, etc. behind the negative forms. Also called a "window" by book format design artists.

Blueline: A final proof made of text pages before they go to press. Changes made at this stage are costly because new negatives must be made and stripped into the flat. Best used to verify pagination.

Boards: The cardboard used as a base for cloth coverings such as found on Casebound books.

C1S: Coated one side, paper stock that has a gloss finish on one side of the sheet. Usually manufactured for use as cover material.

Glossary

C2S: Coated two sides, paper stock that has a gloss finish on both sides of the sheet. Usually manufactured for use as cover material.

Camera Ready: Publisher supplied paper pages ready to shoot or copy with a lithographic camera or reproduction quality scanner.

Casebound: A hard cover book which presents an image of quality such as with library books.

CD: A disc used to archive and protect information.

CD-ROM: A compact disc manufactured with a read-only, or write and read, memory configuration. Considered a very useful form of optical data storage device.

Chokes: When an image is reproduced from a positive and made thinner to prevent color fringing.

CMYK: The colors required to print four-color images similar to a color photograph. Base colors are Cyan, Magenta, Yellow and Black.

Color Key: A color proof which displays an assembled cover in color layers which only approximate the original. Most effective when PMS colors are used.

Glossary

Color Separation: A process wherein the four process colors (CMYK) are separated from a color photograph so they can be output onto negatives for four-color printing press reproduction.

Continuous Tone: The appearance displayed by most photographic prints as defined by the absence of a dot pattern in the picture.

Disk Drive: A device that accepts information from, and writes information onto, hard or floppy disks.

Disk Submission Sheet: The form a publisher should provide the book manufacturer when submitting Disk to Film, Computer to Press, or Print On Demand book publishing projects.

Disk-To-Film: The process by which pages are taken from a publisher's computer disk and imposed on film as a negative from which printing plates will be made.

Disk-To-Paper: The process by which book pages are taken from a publisher's computer disk and printed on paper. See Print On Demand.

Glossary

Document Size: The vertical and horizontal dimensions of the pages which are set up in the computer's application files.

DocuTech: Specific production publishing method using a high-quality digital printer that can copy pages, read electronic files, do collating, stitching, thermal binding, fan folding, halftone production, signatured spread creation, electronic insertion of art and text and file storage.

DPI: Dots Per Inch; the number of dots that can be created within one square inch by an output device or found in a printed reproduction.

Driver: A software program that tells a computer how to run an outside device, such as a printer. One example is a driver that tells the computer to print a Postscript or PDF file onto a disk in the same manner as though it were sending the file to a desktop printer.

Dust Jacket: The color-printed and sometimes laminated cover sheet that wraps around a casebound book. Usually on glossy stock.

End Sheets: Heavy paper stock that is glued onto the inside of the casebound cover and may serve as first and last pages of the book.

Glossary

EPS: Encapsulated Postscript, a graphic format created by an Adobe application to output a book in Postscript printer language commands.

File: A collection of information on a disk, usually either a document or an application.

Filters: An internal software package that is used to decipher and convert files into a form usable between applications. Also known as the conversion program found in word processors.

Final Layout: The last step of book design in which the layout is transferred to the computer to be set up for the laser printer or for output onto a disk.

Final Trim Size: The size of a book when it is bound. For example; 6" by 9" or 8" by 11".

Folio: A word specific for a page number.

Font: Also referred to as typeface. A group of letters, numbers and symbols that share a common type appearance. Fonts are specified by name, weight, and points which define the font's vertical size.

Glossary

Front: The space or margin between the text and the trimmed edge of the book.

Galley: A paper printing of book text which is not yet in page format.

Gloss Lamination: A high-sheen plastic film which is heat-applied to protect the surface of printed covers.

Graphics: Any sort of non-text computer file that is incorporated into or linked to another file. For example: Halftones, logos, photos, line art, etc. Often termed "Art" by book designers.

Halftones: The process of photocopying a continuous tone picture and reproducing the image by imaging it with an overall pattern of a specified percentage and size of dots.

Hard Copy: The paper printout resulting from a computer disk outputting to an active printer.

Hard Disk: A rigid disk and drive that can store and process large amounts of computer data.

Hardware: Components of a computer system.

Head Bands: The strip of colored fabric at the top of the spine as used in casebound books.

Glossary

Icon: A graphic symbol which usually represents a file, folder, disk or computer program.

Justified: Text lines of even length extending to the left and right hand margins of the book pages.

Laser Printer: A common digital printer that creates images by drawing them on a metal drum with a laser beam. The image is then made visible by electrostaticaly attracting dry ink powder to it. This powder image is transferred onto paper and heatset for permanence.

Layout: A proofed drawing that uses ideas from a thumbnail sketch to create a representation of the original design that is suitable for reproduction.

Leading: The space between lines of type on a typeset page, as measured from baseline to baseline of the fonts or typeface used.

Linotronic Driver: A unique set of computer code that creates Postscript files specifically for a Linotronic output device used in production of lithographic film.

Glossary

LPI: Lines Per Inch; the number of lines of text in one vertical inch. Also the number of lines which define the dot pattern of a halftone image.

Margin: The open space from the end, or line, of text to the three trims and gutter of a book.

Matchprint: A method of color proofing which shows an assembled cover almost identical to the way it will appear as four-color printed press output.

Matte Lamination: A dull sheen plastic film which is heat applied to printed covers. Will slightly darken or alter some delicate colors.

Media: The generic name for floppy disks, hard drives, tapes and other devices that store computer data in the form of magnetic impulses. Also related to book marketing.

Modem: A device that enables computers to communicate with each other over the telephone or through internet connections.

Optical Disk: A type of disk for the storage and retrieval of information and graphic files.

Glossary

Outline Font: A font designed for use on a laser printer or typesetter. Rather than being composed of separate dots, like a bit-mapped font, it is made up of an outline of the shape of each letter which can be scaled up or down to any size desired by the book designer.

Page Proof: Laser printer output of how the publisher's final pages will appear when completed with text, folios, headers and footers.

Pagination: A typesetting process wherein the book is partitioned into sequential pages of equal size.

Perfect Binding: Method of adhesively binding a soft cover onto a complete set of page signatures.

Pica: A typesetting measure equal to about 1/6th of an inch and exactly equal to 12 points.

Pixels: The dots displayed to present images on a computer's monitor screen.

Platform: Refers to whether your computer is PC, Macintosh, OS2 or other operating system specific.

Glossary

Plate Ready: Describing negatives supplied by the publisher that have been positioned on a paper flat for plate-making by the book printer.

PMS: Pantone Matching System which describes specific shades of color that are created using various amounts of PMS inks. Each different ink requires is own foundation on the press. PMS colors are identified by specific numbers standardized within the printing industry.

Point: A typesetting measure equal to 1/72nd of an inch. The size of type fonts for printing is typically measured and described in points.

Point Size: The size, measured in points, that a selected typeface will display on the typeset page. Common point sizes used for book text are 9-, 10- and 11-point.

Postscript File: The file output by the Adobe page description language for use by high definition laser printers and typesetters.

Postscript Font: An outline font that works with Postscript and can be resized easily.

Glossary

Postscript Language: A simple, interpretive programming language with powerful graphics capabilities. Its primary application is to establish the appearance of text, graphical shapes and images on printed or displayed pages of computer output sent to a laser-printer or disk.

PPI: Pages Per Inch; a term usually listed when the thickness of book text paper determines the correct spine width and bulk of the book.

Printer Driver: A program file that tells the computer how to send information to a specific type of printer.

Printer Font: The program file that tells the output device how the type font should appear.

Process Screen Match: Similar to PMS colors because they can be built using process colors Cyan, Magenta, Yellow and Black. These colors do not require a separate fountain on the press.

Ragged Factor: Text that is centered on the page with left and right line endings ragged and not justified. Usually used for headlines or inserts.

Glossary

RAM: That part of a computer's memory used for the short-term retention of information, usually until the computer is turned off. Programs and documents may be stored in RAM while you are using them. From "Random Access Memory."

Resolution: The number of dots per inch used to display a graphic image or half-tone image.

ROM: That part of a computer's memory used to store programs which are seldom or never changed. The initials are from "Read Only Memory."

Running Foot: The line at the bottom of a typeset page, known as a "Footer," that may display page number, author's name and/or name of the book, or chapter identification.

Running Head: Line at the top of a typeset page, known as the "Header." It may contain page number, author's name, book title or chapter identification.

Saddle Stitch: A binding method in which cover and text are folded as a unit and stapled together, one or more times, in the center of the fold.

Glossary

Scanner: A machine that converts images into digital form so they can be stored and/or manipulated by a computer graphics program.

Screen Font: A low-resolution, bit-mapped, monitor screen font that mimics a printer's font.

Shareware: Software that is distributed on the honor system, usually through bulletin boards, user groups, information services, etc. You are allowed to try the software and give copies to others. Each user is morally obligated pay a registration fee if they elect to continue using the material after a reasonable trial period.

Software: Computer instruction programs which tell the computer what to do. Also known as programs or software programs.

Spreads: When a lithographic image is reproduced from a negative and in the doing made thicker.

Stock Photography: Photos from an archived file for which cost is determined by the manner of intended use.

Glossary

Style: A variation of a font, such as Italic, Outline, Bold, Shadow, etc. Also format applied to an entire book by the layout artist.

Support Files: Graphics and other material placed inside a file to be output and printed with text.

Thumbnail: A very rough draft design, usually a black and white presentation sketch.

TIFF: From Tagged Information File Format, a standard graphics format for high-resolution bit-mapped images such as generated by scanners.

Tight Registration: Holding the tolerance of printing plates to allow only a minimum of overlap when combining colors or screens.

[This Glossary is courtesy of Gilliland Book Printing,   Arkansas City, Kansas 67005]

References

This list is alphabetized so you can easily find a
   remembered source. But it is not categorized
   because such a list is worth reading from top
   to bottom to learn more of the wide diversity
   of fine services available to the serious self
   publisher in need of additional guidance or
   information.

Amazon.Com, POB 80387, Seattle, Washington
   98108. The internet's major retailer of books
   from all sources.

American Booksellers Association, [800-637-0037] or
   in New York [914-631-7800]. Contact: The
   Publisher Relations Coordinator.

References

Baker & Taylor, Buying Department, POB 8888,
Momence, Il 60954. Supplier to chain and
independent bookstores.

Barnes & Noble, Small Press Department, 122 Fifth
Avenue, New York, N.Y. 10011. Major chain
store and internet retailer of books and
peripherals.

Bookcrafters [734-475-9145] Chelsea, Michigan. A
large book production printer with consistent
quality production of all sizes of books.

Book Marketing & Publicity, 5900 Hollis Street, R2,
Emeryville, California 94608 [800-959-1059]
Newsletter with useful material supporting
book marketing by self publishers.

Book Of Month Club, 1271 Avenue of the Americas,
New York, N.Y. 10020. Has wide variety of
book clubs of all genres. Considers
self-published books.

Book Tech The Magazine 401 North Broad Street,
Philadelphia, Pa 19108 [215-238-5300]
Magazine for printers and book publishing
management.

References

Books In Print R.R.Bowker, 121 Chalon Road, New Providence, NJ 07974 The world's list of practically every book title in print.

Bookwire. A helpful selection of book industry news on the internet. The URL is http://www.bookwire.com

Brodart Co, 500 Arch Street, Williamsport, Pa 17705. A reputable distributor of books from offices located in the eastern United States.

Bradley Communications, 135 E. Plumstead Avenue, Lansdowne, Pennsylvania 19050. Promotes authors through news-letter talk-show publicity directed to radio and television producers.

Copyright Office, Library of Congress, Washington, DC 20559. Where self-publishers write to obtain Form TX to apply for their copyright.

Forthcoming Books In Print R.R.Bowker, 121 Chalon Road, New Providence, NJ 07974. Periodical report of upcoming books. Distributed to libraries and booksellers to encourage pre-orders.

References

Foster & Foster, 104 S. 2nd Street, Fairfield, Iowa 52556. Specialist service in the creation of quality book covers and interior design layouts.

General Learning Corporation, 900 Skokie Boulevard, Northbrook, Il 60062. Nationally known retailer of fine reference and educational books.

Gilliland Printing, 215 North Summit, Arkansas City, Kansas 67005. Mid-western book printer offering a fine variety of short-run services.

Hignell Book Printing, 488 Brunell Street, Winnipeg, Manitoba, Canada R3G 2B4 [800-304-5553] Top quality short run printer providing excellent guidance material and pre-publication data.

Horn Book Magazine 11 Beacon Street, Boston MA, 02108. Carries monthly reviews of children's books. Pre-print galleys are requested.

Ingram Book Company, One Ingram Boulevard, LaVergne, TN 37086. One of nation's largest and best book distributors. Many supportive services.

References

Internal Revenue Service. Telephone [800-829-1040] and request guidelines for authors and publishers.

ISBN Numbers, 121 Chalon Road, New Providence, New Jersey 07974. This group provides ISBN numbers and advises on their correct use.

KNI Inc. [800-886-7301] Anaheim, California. Book production facility located on the West Coast.

Library of Congress, DIP Division, Washington, DC 20540. For maximum sales in the library market you'll need the Library's Preassigned Card Number. Write for an application form.

Lightning Print Inc., 1136 Heil Quaker Road, LaVergne, Tn 37086. Specializes in Print On Demand (POD) with distribution by Ingram Book Company. Also does short runs for publisher marketing.

Lithoid Printing Corporation, 19 Cotters Lane, East Brunswick, N.J. 08816 [908-238-4000] Specializes in short and medium runs for self-publishers.

Lloyd L. Rich, 1163 Vine Street, Denver, Co 80206. Attorney specializing in publication law. Has fine newsletter. URL is www.publaw.com

References

Manual of Style. The University of Chicago Press. LC No. 6-40582 First published 1906. The nation's standard of publishing excellence in typography and book design.

McNaughton & Gunn, Inc., 960 Woodland Drive, Saline, Mi 48176. A full service book manufacturing company in the mid-west.

Premium Incentive Magazine, 1515 Broadway, New York, New York 10036. Possible media for a book review if your title is suitable for their readers who work in the premium marketing field.

Publishers Marketing Association, 2401 Pacific Coast Highway Ste. 102, Hermosa Beach, California 90254. An association for book publishers.

Publishing & Production 401 North Broad Street, Philadelphia, Pa 19108 [215-238-5300] Magazine for major buyers of book printing.

Publishing Mall. Business database about the publishing industry. The URL is http://www.pub-mall.com/

References

Quad/Graphics, N63 W23075 Main Street, Sussex, Wi 53089 [888-782-3226] An award-winning book printer offering a variety of services and books in all sizes and bindings.

Quality Books, 918 Sherwood Drive, Lake Bluff, Illinois 60044. A major distributor of books into public and private libraries.

Robert Howard, 631 Mansfield Drive, Fort Collins, Colorado 80524. Graphic design service, since 1984, for book covers and interior art.

Salesman's Guide, Inc., 1140 Broadway, New York City, New York 10001 Publishes a directory of buyers for premium and incentive products.

Small Publishers Association, 425 Cedar Street, Buena Vista, Colorado 81211. Fine resource for self-publishers offering a valuable newsletter loaded with media and marketing tips.

Sunbelt Publications, 1250 Fayette Street, El Cajon, CA 92020. The west's major distributor of quality regional interest books and calendars.

Thompson-Shore, Inc. 7300 West Joy Road, Dexter, Michigan 48130. From 100 to 20,000 books with in-house binding. Excellent newsletter.

References

Uniform Code Council, 8163 Old Yankee Road, Ste.
  J, Dayton, Ohio 45458. A fine source of
  information on UPC bar codes and their
  numerous uses.

Whitehall Printing Company, 4244 Corporate
  Square, Naples, Fl 34104. A major supplier of
  short-run books since 1959. Has printed
  prices lists for books of common sizes and
  page count.

Index

Index

Index

Index

Index

Index

Self Publishing Made Easy